Michael Stout

MY GAME OF TWO HALVES

MICHAEL STOUT

ISBN 9798695288063

CONTENTS

DEDICATION

To my late dad Felix (1930-1996)

He did not like football and never took me to a match,
but I am eternally grateful that he taught me so many
important values in life and always
encouraged me to do my best.

PRE-MATCH
Two Natural Halves

The dictionary definition of a 'labour of love' is *"something you do because you really want to and not because of any reward you might get for it, even though it involves hard work"*. (www.collinsdictionary.com).

Writing this book was a true labour of love for me. In August 2018, after working mainly in banking for 40 years, I took early retirement. I started to write about my years of following football; catching the football bug aged 7, supporting my local established Football League team (Newcastle United) and hometown non-league team (Gateshead), watching matches in the football mad city of Glasgow where I lived and worked in the 1990s, and many other related events and cultural aspects of The Beautiful Game.

On retiring, I also started non-league groundhopping, with a personal Mission to attend a match at every ground in the two divisions of the Northern League (the world's second oldest league still in existence) and write match reports on them (like a frustrated wannabe football journalist who had missed his vocation earlier in life).

By January 2020, it struck me that I was writing a standard sized book. To be more accurate I was writing one book of two halves – my transformation into a groundhopper in the second half being a marked change from my football watching routine in the first half. It was about the love match that football and I had enjoyed for just over 50 years. It was *My Game of Two Halves*.

They are two unequal halves. The first half covers a period considerably more than the two seasons of the second half, but I believe they are two natural halves of my overall football supporting journey. Mathematicians would of course argue that you cannot have two unequal halves, but this is a book about football not maths.

In March 2020 the coronavirus pandemic saw the United Kingdom go into lockdown and all football was understandably suspended. Extra Time was required in *My Game of Two Halves* to complete my groundhopping Mission.

There have been thousands of books written about football. I have read many of them over the years, and whilst they have certainly influenced my writing, I have not knowingly plagiarised anyone else's work. I have a reasonably good knowledge of the game but I do not claim to be an expert on it. For this book, I have merely selected and written about some of my own personal memories of watching football matches, both as a loyal supporter and a neutral. I am sure other football fans who follow different teams to me will find some empathy with my recollections.

All opinions are my own personal ones and are open to be agreed or disagreed with. One of the best things about football is that, by its varied nature, it fosters diverse views that rational fans tolerate in the common love of the game.

The players have shaken hands and are now in their positions raring to go. The crowd are expectant. The referee blows his whistle and my labour of love, My Game of Two Halves, kicks off.

I hope you enjoy reading it.

Michael Stout

Newcastle-upon-Tyne, England

October 2020

THE FIRST HALF

My Long-Term Relationship with Football

CHAPTER

A DEDICATED FOLLOWER OF FOOTBALL

Football.

The beautiful game.

I watch football and I am not alone. I am just one of millions of like-minded individuals, all of whom will have a different story to tell about how they caught the football bug and how their love of the game developed over the years.

Attending match days and match nights.

In all kinds of good and bad weather.

With the many and the few.

Experiencing the highs and lows. The joys and woes.

In the stands and on the terraces of stadia of all shapes and sizes.

Plus countless hours watching it on television, both in pubs and at home on the comfort of the sofa.

Football is sociable, exciting, dramatic and enjoyable escapism. It can also be at times tedious, frustrating and heart-breaking.

In my opinion, it is indeed **THE** beautiful game.

FOOTBALL FANATICS

In 1979, a half hour comedy called Golden Gordon aired on BBC Television. Written by Michael Palin and Terry Jones from the Monty Python satirical comedy team, it starred Palin as Gordon Ottershaw – a fanatical supporter of hapless Barnstoneworth United FC, who had not won a match for 6 years. After a heavy 8-bloody-1 defeat, Gordon heads back home to smash all the furniture in anger. He wears his Barnstoneworth scarf in bed. He named his son Barnstoneworth. He is totally obsessed with the club - so much so that he never hears his wife's many fruitless attempts throughout the programme to tell him she is going to have a baby. As well as being very funny, it is a great parody of football fanaticism.

Like Gordon, there are some people who could rightly be described as football fanatics (maybe not quite as extreme though).

There are the supporters who attend every match their team plays, home and away. It would take something extremely important for them to miss one; for example, the birth of their child or having to rest and recuperate after a major operation. In some cases however these would still not be definite reasons to miss travelling to Azerbaijan by plane, train or whatever means available, to watch the team they support in a fairly pointless pre-season friendly.

There are the groundhoppers, who travel far and wide attending matches at as many different grounds as possible. They will usually keep meticulous records of every ground they 'tick off'. Details could include score, scorers, attendance, bookings, red cards, price of admission, price of chips and curry sauce, and marks out of ten for the half-time pies.

There are the supporters who sing non-stop at a match. Usually fuelled by alcohol, they can often go for the full 90 minutes delivering a medley of their favourite chants; sometimes in tune and sometimes out of tune (particularly towards the end of the second half when, like some of the players on the pitch, they are starting to tire). Sometimes they will just sing the same short chant over and over for the whole match. They also goad their own fans in other sections of the ground for not singing. Their love of exercising their vocal chords can of course be annoying to other fans sitting nearby who just want to watch the match in peace, but the singers' support for their team can only be admired and applauded in my opinion. Options for non-singers who want to make a constant noise during a match include bass drums, trumpets and, for a short period after the 2010 South African World Cup, vuvuzelas.

There are also The Collectors. Most clubs change their shirt designs every season or two and some fans will religiously buy the new shirt every time it changes. Some will also buy the away strip and, if their club is playing in European competition, the third strip (that will likely be bright pink and yellow hoops or something equally as hideous). Other fans have complete collections of programmes from all the matches they have been to, lovingly stored in perfect chronological order.

I salute these groups of enthusiasts, who clearly spend more time and money following football than I do. I have friends who fall into the categories above and I call them fanatics with total respect for what they do.

FOOTBALL ATTRACTION

I would describe myself as a football fan rather than a football fanatic; occasional rather than obsessive. From an early age I have always been interested in the game. I played it, albeit at a relatively friendly lower level and not at a competitive higher level, until I physically had to stop when I reached my mid-fifties. There have been times when watching football has taken a bit of a back seat for me; for example, when relationships must take priority, or during very busy periods at work, or when I have been pursuing some of my other interests (hillwalking for example). It feels like I have had, and am still having, a long-term relationship with football that is sometimes a bit rocky, rather than being completely married to it. I have strayed at times to watch other sports - rugby, cricket, athletics and golf – but I have always returned to my first sporting love of football, with a grovelling apology and a metaphorical bunch of flowers. I have made a long-term commitment without actually taking The Football Marriage Vows.

'Do you take this football team to be your faithfully supported team, to love and to scold, from this day forward, in Premier League and Championship, and even if things go really wrong and they drop into non-league; for richer and for poorer (more likely poorer given the cost of season tickets, replica strips etc), until death (or until you just get completely sick of their boring negative tactics) you do part?'

So, what is the attraction of football? And why do we spend so much time, energy and money watching 22 men or women knocking a ball around a piece of grass? Here is what I think are the main reasons;

- *It is an escape from your normal routine*

After the stresses and strains (or maybe tedium) of a week at work or college, going to a football match at the weekend allows you to switch off from your usual routine for a short time. For an hour and a half you can forget about any weekday worries and be entertained by some footballers – hopefully that is. I say hopefully because unlike some forms of escapism (e.g. going to a cinema to watch the latest film release or going to a theatre to watch a play or a band) where you basically know what you are going to get for your money, with football no two matches are the same so you cannot always guarantee that you will be entertained. All football fans have been to certain matches that were so dull that they wished they had not bothered to make the effort to attend. Generally though knowing that you will be able to watch a football match at the weekend makes the daily grind during the week seem a bit more bearable.

- *It allows you to avoid doing other stuff you do not like*

After your busy working week, the weekend gives you the dubious pleasure of doing some of the stuff that you have not had time to do during the week. This stuff can include shopping (both for food and just being dragged around against your will looking at things in multiple shops), painting/decorating, and if you have children taking them to do activities that are interesting to them (but are not particularly interesting to you). There may be some pressure from another party (e.g. wife, husband, girlfriend, boyfriend, son, daughter) to make this stuff a priority on a match day. This is no time for a faint heart. You need to toughen up and ensure going to watch football takes precedence. If you cannot absolve yourself totally from doing this other stuff on a match day, careful planning is required to ensure you can complete this stuff and still attend the match. For example, if on a Saturday your wife insists you have to choose between taking your daughter to ballet classes in the morning or badminton lessons in the afternoon, plump for the ballet, where (assuming a 3pm kick off) you can do your fatherly duty in the morning and then make it to the pub in time for a couple of pre-match pints with your mate. Shopping and painting/decorating avoidance is more difficult to achieve consistently, but where possible do not plan to do this stuff when your team has a home match; if possible only do it on a weekend when your team has an away match with a 400 mile plus round trip that, if pushed, you do not really mind missing.

- *It is an uncomplicated game*

Football is uncomplicated? Most managers and coaches will disagree, citing all the detailed tactical planning that is needed before and during matches. For the football fan though I believe it is uncomplicated compared to most sports. Football matches last 90 minutes plus a small but variable amount of added time (and of course there are occasions in cup competitions where 30 minutes extra time and even penalties happen). Unlike some golf tournaments and test or county cricket matches though, you do not have to set aside four full days of your time to find out who wins. In less than two hours you will have a result in a football match. The winning team will quite simply be the team that has put the ball, by legal means, into their opponents' net the most times. Ball in the net = 1 goal, most goals scored wins; if both teams score the same number of goals the match is drawn. And that is it. There are no complicated scoring systems in football unlike, for example, rugby where the points awarded vary depending on whether the team has scored a try, a conversion, a penalty or a drop goal. There is also a lot more brain power required to work out how to win a game of darts (adding and subtracting in your head, working out doubles and trebles) or snooker (adding up red balls and different valued coloured balls potted in a break, and working out how many points you need to score to leave your opponent requiring snookers). There are no such mathematical brain teasers in the game of football. If your football team is drawing 1-1, it is straightforward to work out that they need to score just one more goal and not concede to win. Also, there are no bonus points or run rates to factor into football league tables - 3 points are awarded for winning a match and 1 point for a draw. It is uncomplicated and I for one like it that way.

- *It is very sociable and gives you a sense of belonging*

I think it is fair to say that we are heavily influenced by others in choosing what football team to support. Often at a young impressionable age, football fans will follow the same team as older family members or friends, and usually this is the local team. This is no bad thing as you develop pride in your local area, then loyalty to your local football team and you gain a sense of identity. You can attend matches with like-minded individuals who all want to see your team win and you can enjoy all the pre- and post-match camaraderie that goes with it. When your team is winning and playing entertaining football it is a great feeling and you can all celebrate it together. When your team is playing badly and not doing very well, you have your fellow supporters who are all in the same boat to console you. You will support your team through thick and thin. Even when they are going through a bad patch you will not want to miss a home game in case the one you do not go to is an absolute classic - the very one where they turn the corner and win 6-0.

I accept that not everyone chooses to support a local team though. The decision to support a team from outside of your local area is usually based on their higher level of success and/or they have some world class players. Popular choices are Manchesters United and City, Chelsea, Liverpool and Arsenal. If you live in Hartlepool but do not want to follow Hartlepool United, you are more likely to choose the multiple trophy winning Manchester United than, with respect, the less glamorous Crewe Alexandra. The downside of living in Hartlepool and supporting

Manchester United is that going to watch your team will cost significantly more, if indeed you are even able to acquire a ticket for Old Trafford given the huge demand. Looking a bit further afield, young children in the UK who support Barcelona with their Messi 10 shirts will need to study hard at school and university to try to secure the well-paid job they will need in adulthood to be able to afford to travel to Spain to watch their team every week. I believe that following your local team will usually give you more of a sense of belonging and comradeship than following a distant team of superstars, but even these glory hunter fans are alright by me – anyone who loves football is to be honest.

FOOTBALL FOLLOWER

My own initial attraction to football started in the late 1960s and fifty years or so later it is still going strong. It certainly has earned the right to be called a long-term relationship. The 1960s English rock band The Kinks had a hit single called Dedicated Follower of Fashion around the time I was becoming interested in football. It could never be said that I am a dedicated follower of fashion, but when it comes to dedicatedly following football, that is a different matter.

CHAPTER

TWO SIDES OF THE TYNE

I grew up supporting two football teams – Newcastle United and Gateshead. They have never played in the same league and are usually at least four leagues apart. It seems very unlikely that they ever will compete in the same league so supporting both has always been possible and has felt reasonable.

The city of Newcastle upon Tyne is situated on the north bank of the River Tyne and the town of Gateshead is situated on the south bank. This North East of England city and town have been constant features throughout my life.

I was born in Gateshead, attended junior school there and, after passing the now defunct Eleven Plus examination in 1972, attended secondary grammar school in Newcastle.

I lived in Gateshead during my childhood and early adulthood and have lived for the last two decades in Newcastle.

I attained a Business Studies qualification at Gateshead Technical College in 1979 and a Post Graduate Diploma with Distinction in Management Studies from Northumbria University, Newcastle in 2003.

After leaving school, my first job was at a bank based in Newcastle, where I changed from travelling via two buses from Gateshead to Newcastle to school five days a week, to making a similar journey to work five days a week.

As a keen lover of live music, I regularly watched (and often jumped around and sweated to) bands at Newcastle City Hall and Newcastle Mayfair in the late 1970s and 1980s. Now I am more at home watching bands in the comfort of the magnificent Sage Gateshead music venue.

Gateshead was once regarded as a dirty back lane leading to Newcastle, but that can hardly be said about it now. Following the decline of shipbuilding, the regeneration of the River Tyne has produced the aforementioned Sage Gateshead concert hall and the Baltic Centre for Contemporary Art. There are seven bridges across the Tyne between Newcastle and Gateshead, the most recently constructed being the award-winning Gateshead Millennium Bridge for pedestrians and cyclists that opened in 2001. Also located in Gateshead, about four miles from the River Tyne, is Antony Gormley's contemporary 20-metre-high steel sculpture The Angel of the North, erected in 1998. These buildings and structures have become tourist attractions and enabled Gateshead to shake off the dirty back lane tag. Indeed, since 2000 the two Councils, in conjunction with more than 100 private sector organisations in North East England, established the NewcastleGateshead Initiative, to market and develop the area for the mutual benefit of both Newcastle and Gateshead, and forge closer links between the two.

My personal links to the north and south sides of the River Tyne have clearly nurtured my support of the two footballing sides of the Tyne for the past half century.

MY FIRST MATCHES

I was 7 years old when I watched a full game of football for the first time. It was the FA Cup Final on television.

Saturday 18th May 1968
West Bromwich Albion 1 Everton 0
BBC Television (Live from Wembley Stadium, London)

I watched it intently even though I had no allegiance, then or now, to either team. Up until then, the most exciting television I had watched as a young boy was Gerry Anderson's Thunderbirds. I was always on the edge of seat watching an episode of this, wondering whether the Tracy brothers of International Rescue were going to be able to save people on an out of control aircraft or trapped underwater in a sunken boat or drifting in a space rocket on a crash course for the sun (they always did of course). I was now on the edge of my seat watching live football on television, and like Thunderbirds, there was plenty of tension. I was glued to the television set for over two hours (West Bromwich Albion won the Cup via a Jeff Astle goal in extra time).

Like many football fans, my introduction to the game was being taken as a youngster to a match by an adult. My dad went against the grain of those times - he was a working man who was not keen on football. My grandad and uncle however were avid Gateshead fans, so when I started to show an interest in football at that tender age, it was agreed that I could go with them to a match. They had watched Gateshead regularly for over 20 years, during the club's football league years playing in the English League Third Division North in the 1950s and the non-league years after being voted out of the Football League in 1960. For the 1968/69 season the club had joined the newly formed Northern Premier League that at the time was, together with the Southern Premier League, the highest level in non-league football. My first live football match was also Gateshead's first match in the Northern Premier League; at the Redheugh Park ground that had been their home since 1930.

Saturday 10th August 1968
Gateshead 0 South Liverpool 0
Redheugh Park, Gateshead

I cannot remember much about the actual match. This is of course partly due to being only 7 years old but could also be because the match finished goalless (and I am assuming may not have been a thrilling contest). Bizarrely though I can remember a lot of other details about the day. Even though it was summertime, my mam had made me wear a coat and scarf (just in case the weather changed). I was given a bag of salted peanuts to eat. The pre-match entertainment was a local rock band, sporting the long hair and flared trousers that were in vogue at that time, playing on the pitch (with the benefit of hindsight this was quite strange given that the sparse but faithful crowd were in the more mature age group that was unlikely to appreciate rock music). The pitch was surrounded by a greyhound track and there was a large scoreboard used for the greyhound racing behind one of the goals. The stadium had a capacity of over 20,000 but the days of thousands of fans attending had gone. There were only a few hundred diehards gathered in the main stand at this match. I took a walk with my uncle around the stadium during the match, slowly strolling around the empty covered terraces on the other side of the pitch opposite the main stand and behind the goals. He told me of the days in the 1950s when these terraces were packed. This was a club that had clearly seen better times but it was also my hometown team and I knew then that I would always support Gateshead. I also knew that my first experience of the big match atmosphere (although I accept that small match atmosphere might be a more accurate description) would not be my last. I had caught the football bug.

I continued to go to games at Redheugh Park during the 1968/69 season with my grandad and uncle. I watched Gateshead do battle with Hyde United and Netherfield amongst others, and with more local rivals Ashington and South Shields. At the end of the 1968/69 season, Brian Clough brought his Derby County team to

Redheugh Park for a friendly to raise some much needed funds for Gateshead FC. The club had clearly secured this lucrative match due to Clough's strong North East connections. He was born in and played for Middlesbrough. He also played for Sunderland until his career was cut short at 29 years old with a bad anterior cruciate ligament injury. Derby had just been promoted to the First Division of the Football League after winning the Second Division title. As expected they beat Gateshead (for the record it was 5-0) but the result was immaterial – more importantly there was a good crowd, well above the typical attendance at a Northern Premier League game. My most abiding memory of it was when the ball went out of play behind Derby's goal and landed near me. I picked it up and saw that Derby's goalkeeper Les Green was right in front of me, having ran behind his goal to collect the ball. I passed him the ball and he said 'thanks'. This was the closest I had ever been to a professional footballer and it felt very exciting at the time as an 8-year-old football fan.

(One amazing fact about Gateshead FC is that they are the only team in England to have a 100% win record against Liverpool. To be fair they have only met once in a competitive match though – a 1-0 Gateshead victory in the FA Cup 3rd Round in 1953).

THE VASE AND TWO BANANAS

As exciting as this was, there was a great deal more excitement during the 1968/69 season on the north side of the Tyne, as Newcastle United made their debut in a European competition. On Wednesday 29th May 1968, eleven days after the West Brom v Everton FA Cup Final, I watched the European Cup Final that was also broadcast live on BBC Television. Manchester United became the first English team to win Europe's top prize, beating Benfica of Portugal 4-1 after extra time. I was pleased that an English team had won the European Cup and particularly enjoyed watching George Best and Bobby Charlton. Unlike some of my school friends I did not however become a lifelong Manchester United fan. My allegiances have always been to my two sides of the Tyne.

In the 1968/69 season, Newcastle United were given the opportunity to emulate this European success. At the end of the 1967/68 season they finished 10th in the First Division but fortuitously they were still one of 4 English clubs entered into 1968/69's Inter Cities Fairs Cup. This was the European competition, more commonly known as the Fairs Cup, that became the UEFA Cup and later the Europa League. At this time, there was a rule that only one club per city could take part to win this trophy, that looked like a silver vase with two bananas for handles. This meant that Liverpool who finished 3rd in the First Division at the end of the 1967/68 season were entered but their same city rivals Everton who finished 5th were not. 6th placed Chelsea represented the City of London but Tottenham Hotspur (7th) and Arsenal (9th) missed out. Newcastle certainly struck lucky to qualify for their first European adventure but once they did they took the completion very seriously indeed.

My 8-year-old self was oblivious to their extremely fortunate route into the Fairs Cup and I was too young to attend any of the matches during the campaign. I mainly followed the team's progress from match reports in the local daily newspaper (the Newcastle Evening Chronicle) and from word of mouth accounts from friends who were a few years older and lucky enough and presumably considered to be old enough, to be taken to St James Park by their fathers to watch the home legs. When the Chronicle arrived the evening after a Fairs Cup match I would, once my mam had read the Births, Marriages and Deaths Notices (the hatched, matched and dispatched), devour the back pages - reading the match report, analysis and statistics, and looking at the grainy black and white photographs of the action.

The young Newcastle team were not expected to advance very far, but on Thursday 29th May 1969 at 7.30 pm they were running out at their St James' Park home ground in front of a 60,000 crowd for the First Leg of the Final against Ujpest Dozsa of Hungary. They had defeated some of Europe's biggest clubs at the time on the way – Feyenoord Rotterdam of Holland, Sporting Lisbon of Portugal, Real Zaragoza of Spain, Vitoria Setubal of Portugal, and in the Semi Final Glasgow Rangers (2-0 on aggregate in what can best be described as a feisty two legged affair). I watched the highlights of the First Leg of the Final when it was shown later the same evening on BBC Television. On a black and white TV (that my parents rented from Rediffusion) I watched the black and white striped shirts of Newcastle United win 3-0, with 2 goals from captain Bobby Moncur (63 and 72 minutes) and Jim Scott (83 minutes). Incredibly these were the first goals Moncur (a defensive wing half) had scored in 7 years at the club. Younger readers may like to seek out and view footage of the match on YouTube (warning – picture quality is about as far removed from Sky Sports Ultra HD as you can get).

Two weeks later I was allowed to stay up late on a school night to listen to the Second Leg on the radio (there was no live TV coverage). It was broadcasted via satellite from Budapest. Midway through the first half, with the score goalless, the satellite signal went down, so I sat in radio silence waiting for it to return. When it was restored again during the half time interval, I was shocked to hear that Ujpest Dozsa were leading 2-0, meaning it was now only 3-2 to Newcastle on aggregate. It is said that manager Joe Harvey's team talk was simply along the lines of 'go back out, score a goal and we've won it'. Within a minute of the restart, in true Roy of the Rovers' style (younger readers may want to Google this phrase) Moncur did just that. Further goals by Ben Arentoft (50 minutes) and Alan Foggon (74 minutes) sealed the victory, 3-2 on the night and 6-2 on aggregate. Cue my 8-year-old self running around the house, cheering and waving my black and white striped scarf (hand knitted by my mam) – and being quickly told to go to bed because I had school in the morning.

Wednesday 11th June 1969
Ujpest Dozsa 2 Newcastle United 3
Listening on the Radio
(Satellite broadcast from Megyeri Uti Stadium, Budapest, Hungary)

The next day at school I was euphoric. One of my teams had beaten the rest of Europe and won the Fairs Cup. I joined my Newcastle United supporter friends in the schoolyard taunting the carpet bagging-type kids who supported the United team based 150 miles away in Manchester. I could have been forgiven for thinking back then that Newcastle would go on to win more and more trophies and I would regularly have that same jubilant feeling again, but 50 years later they have still not won another significant trophy since that night in Budapest when Bobby Moncur held the vase and two bananas aloft.

When Moncur retired from football one of the jobs he had was managing a Squash Club in Gateshead. In 1984 I was at an evening function there, and felt it did not seem right when the captain of the 1969 Fairs Cup winning team was collecting empty glasses from our table. In the modern era of vastly greater financial rewards to players during their football careers, it is highly unlikely that more recent captains of English clubs winning European trophies (e.g. Stephen Gerrard of Liverpool in 2005 and John Terry of Chelsea in 2012) will ever need to do this.

GANNIN' TO TOON

Although Newcastle is a city, locals often refer to going into the city centre as 'going to the town' or in the Geordie dialect 'gannin to the toon'. Newcastle United Football Club became known as The Toon and the fans became known as The Toon Army. (Similarly the Geordie pronunciation of Gateshead is 'Gatesheed', Gateshead Football Club are known as The Heed and the fans are known as The Heed Army).

I attended some Gateshead matches with my grandad and uncle during the late 1960s and early 1970s but the club was struggling due to lack of finances and had dropped down to a much lower level of non-league football. In the same period, Newcastle United were playing in the top level of English football (League Division One) and were regular occupants of mid-table positions. As a youngster gradually becoming more and more interested in playing and watching football, it was inevitable that I was drawn to the comparatively more glamorous football that Newcastle United were playing on the north side of the Tyne.

Wednesday 12th September 1973
Newcastle United 3 Ipswich Town 1
St James Park, Newcastle-upon-Tyne

Given my dad's lack of interest in football, it was with his blessing that a work colleague of his took me to my first Newcastle United match. On Wednesday 12th September 1973, I was one of a crowd of over 30,000 at St James' Park who watched Newcastle beat Ipswich Town 3-1 (2 goals from Malcolm 'Supermac' Macdonald and an own goal). Compared to the Gateshead matches I had attended, this was a far more exciting experience, with more atmosphere and much more crowd noise. There were also more star players on the pitch, whose photos I had in my Soccer Stars in Action Picture Stamp Album. (Older readers will remember collecting these action photos of players from the 22 English First Division teams and sticking them in an album). Apart from Supermac, there was his striking partner John Tudor (when The Toon fans sang 'Hallelujah John Tudor' I thought it was the greatest chant ever at the time), Terry McDermott (who went on to win 3 European Cup winners' medals with Liverpool in 1977, 1978 and 1981) and Frank Clark (who after playing most of his long career at Newcastle, incredibly won a European Cup winners' medal with Nottingham Forest in his last ever competitive match in 1979).

My dad had told his work colleague to curb his swearing. He managed to do this for about five minutes before shouting at the referee and questioning his parentage. He continued in this vein for the rest of the evening. He told me not to mention any of this to my dad. I learnt from him, like thousands of other young fans have been told and will continue to be told, that what happens at the match stays at the match.

A few weeks later, on Saturday 13th October 1973 to be precise, I went back to St James' Park with a friend from school to watch Newcastle play Manchester City. At the Ipswich match I was in the relative safety and calm of the Paddock (the standing area at the side of the pitch opposite the dugouts) but this time I was in the Gallowgate End and this was a totally different animal. This was the area of the ground with the cheapest price of admission. It was a large standing only sloping terrace located behind one of the goals with concrete crush barriers at various levels of it. We stood right behind the goal at the bottom of the terracing and this gave us a perfect view of Malcolm Macdonald's shot hitting the back of the net after 23 minutes. Even though I had been to a few football matches by this time, the moment the net bulged right in front of us and Supermac wheeled away punching the air whilst being congratulated by his team mates, was when I really truly fell head over heels in love with the sport. The goal prompted the fans in the Gallowgate End to surge forwards in celebration, and along with a few other teenage Toon fans we had to jump over the low wall at the bottom of the terrace and onto the cinder track behind the goal to avoid being literally being thrown head over heels.

I had seriously caught the football bug now. I regularly attended games at St James' Park and Gateshead International Stadium (their new home after Redheugh Park was demolished in 1972) during the 1970s and 1980s. Surprisingly, with my great penchant for record keeping, I have not kept a record of all the Newcastle United and Gateshead home games I have been to over the last 50 years but it is certainly in triple figures for both sides.

I was in love with football but to paraphrase Shakespeare 'the course of true love of a football team (or teams) doesn't always run smooth'.

CHAPTER

100 YEARS OF HURT

I've been hurting for a century?

It is of course only half a century, but when your two sides of the Tyne have both gone 50 years without any major success, often falling right at the last hurdle, it feels appropriate to double the pain and call it 100 years.

There are only a small number of what I would define as major trophies to win in English football – the Premier League title, the FA Cup and the Football League Cup (in its many sponsored guises – the energy drink Carabao being the current one). These trophies are usually won by a handful of the bigger/bigger spending Premier League clubs meaning most football fans are truly fortunate if their team wins one of these trophies. For example, loyal Wigan Athletic fans, who followed their amazing rise from non-league to Premier League, must have still never expected them to win the FA Cup, but they did just that in 2013. When Liverpool won the Premier League title in 2019/20 for the first time since 1989/90, it was heralded as putting an end to 30 years of failure. During these so-called years of failure they had won 2 European Cups, the UEFA Cup, 3 FA Cups and 4 League Cups. Newcastle United supporters would gladly take that kind of failure instead of the real failure of not winning anything significant for 50 years.

THE 1970s

WEMBLEY WOES (PART 1)

Newcastle reached, and lost, two domestic cup finals in the 1970s. They played Liverpool in the 1974 FA Cup Final at Wembley. As an excited 13-year-old, I watched the match as it was broadcast live on TV. My parents now had a colour television and I draped my black and white striped scarf over it in eager anticipation of a Toon triumph. Sadly the performance of the boys in the black and white stripes was anything but colourful on the day, as Liverpool ran out easy 3-0 winners. (Kevin Keegan scored two of the Liverpool goals – he was to become a future villain turned hero for Newcastle United). In the 1976 League Cup Final they lost 2-1 to Manchester City after another poor forgettable Wembley performance. As sad as losing a Cup Final is, things deteriorated further when Newcastle were relegated from the top flight at the end of the 1977/78 season.

Things were much worse for my side on the south bank of the Tyne though. Financial difficulties in the early years of the 1970s saw Gateshead FC enter liquidation in 1974. South Shields FC, who did not have their own ground, relocated to Gateshead for the 1974/75 season. Renamed as Gateshead United, the team competed in the Northern Premier League, playing their home games at the Gateshead International Stadium (commonly known as the GIS). The pitch has a running track around it and at that time the GIS was primarily an athletics venue (I watched Brendan Foster of Gateshead Harriers, the well-known middle distance athlete who later founded the Great North Run, break the 3,000 metres world record at the stadium in 1974).

I was a regular attendee at the GIS in the mid to late 1970s – I went there more than going to St James' Park during that period. My dad made me a banner with 'Howay The Lads – Gateshead United' on it, that was held together with two heavy wooden poles. My brother, friends and I used to take it to every home game, taking turns to carry it due to its substantial weight. The stewards were a bit wary of it at the first match we took it to, but when we assured them that it was not an offensive weapon, they let us parade it on the running track and we got a round of applause from the few hundred supporters in the main stand. My two favourite players of this era were Kenny Heslop and Les Mutrie. Heslop was a small tricky winger with a good burst of pace. Mutrie was a giant striker with impressive big sideburns that gave Noddy Holder of Slade and Alvin Stardust (similar mutton chopped pop stars at that time) a run for their money. He went on to play for Hull City in the Football League during the early 1980s, partnering Billy Whitehurst.

In 1977, Gateshead had another financial scare and subsequent rescue by two local businessmen who were lifelong supporters. The club spent the rest of the decade in the Northern Premier League (2 levels below the Football League).

THE TUNNEL

One brief shining moment in the general doom and gloom at the GIS happened on a cold December evening in 1975. Gateshead were playing Rochdale from Football League Division 4 in the 2nd Round of the FA Cup. Instead of the usual few hundred home supporters, there were an estimated 10,000 in the GIS that night, most of whom had not paid to get in. Some climbed over the stadium's relatively low outer walls, and some surged in just before kick-off when the stewards decided to open the main gates to avoid people being potentially crushed in the large crowd queuing up outside. For the record, my friends and I did not go over the wall or through the gates – we actually went under the wall via a small tunnel under the fence at the back of the terracing behind one of the goals. We had used it a few times previously (sorry Gateshead FC but we were poor teenagers) and we continued to use it for a few more matches after this one until we were spotted by a steward before a particular match. We were reprimanded, the tunnel was subsequently blocked up and we paid to enter all future games via the turnstiles. It was an exciting and close cup tie, but when Rochdale took the lead things were looking bleak. However, a great late goal by Ron Guthrie (who had an FA Cup winner's medal from the 1973 Final when playing for Sunderland against Leeds United) earned Gateshead a replay (that Rochdale won 3-1).

Monday 15th December 1975
Gateshead 1 Rochdale 1
Gateshead International Stadium, Gateshead, Tyne and Wear

Many of the crowd, including myself, invaded the pitch at the end. With the unusually large crowd and a good result against a higher-level club, there was quite rightly a celebratory mood at the final whistle, but it would be another 34 years supporting Gateshead before I had that exalted feeling again.

THE 1980s

During the 1980s I was in my twenties and working in a clerical job at a bank. This type of employment was often called a job for life back then – how things have changed. I was earning a decent steady wage, enabling me to continue going to matches at both sides of the Tyne. I had other interests in my twenties though, with consequent drains on my finances. I attended a lot of live music concerts, did a lot of hillwalking (mainly in the Lake District and Scotland) and did a lot of socialising in pubs and nightclubs. The other interests meant I could be best described as a fairly regular supporter of both clubs during this decade – not a 'go every Saturday without fail' one.

WE LET THE STARS GO

Newcastle United started the decade in the Second Division. There was little to shout about in the first few seasons of the 1980s but there was suddenly a real buzz in the 1983/84 season. Under manager Arthur Cox, and with young up and coming local lads Chris Waddle and Peter Beardsley, and ex-England captain Kevin Keegan as the core of the team, The Toon finished in 3rd place and won promotion back to the First Division. The feel-good factor was definitely back at St James Park that season. It was a joy to watch Beardsley jinking around defenders and scoring some beautiful goals; Waddle collecting a pass on the halfway line and tearing down the wing leaving opponents for dead; and Keegan 'the orchestra leader' showing why he had been at the top of the game for so long. I was so caught up in the excitement of the promotion push that I went to my first Newcastle away match (versus Charlton Athletic at The Valley on Saturday 7th April 1984 to see a 3-1 Toon win) with some friends. As much as it felt great to be promoted, I never class this as a major success; merely it is putting right the ignominy of being relegated in the first place.

At 33 years of age, Keegan retired from football at the end of this season, deciding to conclude his very successful career on a bit of a high rather than maybe struggling with the faster pace of the First Division again. After his final match at St James Park he was flown in a helicopter from the pitch still wearing his full kit.

Without setting the world on fire, Newcastle maintained their First Division status for a few seasons. Another exciting local youngster from Dunston (village in Gateshead), Paul 'Gazza' Gascoigne made his debut in 1985. He was effectively a replacement for Chris Waddle who was sold to Tottenham Hotspur in July 1985. Lack of funds, the start of a boardroom takeover bid and supporter unrest at the sale of key players (as well as Waddle, Peter Beardsley was sold to Liverpool in 1987 and Gazza himself was sold to Tottenham Hotspur in 1989) were main features of the second half of the 1980s. Prefab Sprout, a popular music band from the North East of England, recorded a song called We Let The Stars Go in 1990. It was not about Newcastle selling all their star players, but for a brief spell it became synonymous on Tyneside with Waddle et al leaving. The decade finished in a familiar way to the 1970s, with Newcastle relegated to the Second Division at the end of the 1988/89 season.

HEEDING UP AND DOWN

Gateshead established themselves in the Northern Premier League in the early 1980s. They won this league in the 1982/83 season with 100 points and 114 goals from 42 games – 16 points ahead of 2nd placed Mossley – and were promoted to the Alliance Premier League. This was a great achievement, but my yardstick of real success for Gateshead will always only be a return to the Football League. It meant that they were now one step below the Football League but there was no automatic promotion to it. Instead, the League clubs voted on whether the Alliance winners could replace one of the bottom 4 teams in the Fourth Division, and usually the old pals act worked against non-league teams achieving their dream. Sadly, in 1960, Gateshead were one of the few Football League teams that were not re-elected this way (they were 3rd from bottom of the Fourth Division but were considered too northerly for the higher proportion of Southern England teams in the League at that time, and the greyhound track around Redheugh Park was frowned upon). In the 1980s, Gateshead's squad was part time and striker Keith McNall worked with me at the bank. If he had a Tuesday night long journey away game (at for example Yeovil or Maidstone), I would do most of his work for him the next day, as he was often half asleep due to only getting back home in the early hours of Wednesday morning (probably after scoring one or more of the 105 league goals he scored in his Heed career). I was always happy to help my hometown team in any way of course! To be fair Keith would return the favour for me sometimes.

During the second half of the 1980s, Gateshead were a yo-yo club between the top and second tiers of non-league football. They had two relegations with subsequent quick promotions, finishing the decade in the top tier.

There had been highs and lows watching my two sides of the Tyne during the 1980s, but the real glittering prizes were still elusive for both.

THE 1990s

For the majority of the 1990s I lived and worked in Glasgow. A combination of practical, financial and geographical reasons meant I went to Newcastle and Gateshead home matches very infrequently, watching football in Glasgow instead (recounted in Chapter 5 of this book).

SPELL IN TOP TIER ENDS IN TEARS

Gateshead spent most of this decade in the top tier of non-league football. This was now called the Football Conference with the league winners gaining automatic promotion to the Football League (providing their ground was up to scratch). Gateshead consolidated their position at this level for 8 seasons, finishing in mainly mid to lower half of the league table positions (exceptions to this were a 7th place finish in 1994/95 and a 5th place finish in 1995/96). On the few occasions I did go to the GIS to watch them during this period they played some good football but they never looked like seriously challenging for the automatic promotion place. The end of the 1997/98 saw them finish 2nd bottom of the Conference and they were relegated to the Northern Premier League.

THE RETURN OF THE KING

My north side of the Tyne started the 1990s in the Second Division. Before I moved to Glasgow in June 1992, I still regularly went to Newcastle matches, including memorable away days at Barnsley and Bradford City, but the early 1990s were dark times for The Toon. Optimism returned when local millionaire businessman Sir John Hall took ownership of the club after a bitter boardroom battle. The storm clouds lifted further in February 1992 when Hall appointed Kevin 'King Kev' Keegan as manager. On Saturday 8th February 1992, my friend Alan and I went to Keegan's first match in charge. The local media were referring to it in biblical terms - The Return of the Messiah and The Prodigal Son is Back type stuff. The pubs in Newcastle city centre were full of Toon fans pre-match and the atmosphere was electric; the recent doom and gloom lifted by the mere anticipation that Keegan, in his first managerial role, might be able to help bring back the good times. After a couple of pints in a pub near to St James' Park, we arrived at the ground about an hour before kick-off and stood on the packed Gallowgate End terrace, chanting Keegan's name with the rest of the fans there. When Keegan emerged just before kick-off, the whole ground erupted.

As understandable as all of this euphoria was, it was at odds with the predicament Newcastle United were in at this stage of the 1991/92 season. They were lying second from bottom of Division 2 with only 6 wins from 30 games, and only one win in the last 11 games. They were in real danger of dropping into the third tier of English football for the first time ever. The fans had been voting with their feet so far this season, with home attendances reducing to the 15,000 – 20,000 range. This would have been unthinkable a few seasons earlier. The official attendance for Keegan's first match as manager was significantly higher at 29,263.

After all the pre-match razzmatazz was over, the reality of needing a result against fellow relegation strugglers Bristol City kicked in. The crowd were tense and the players seemed tense, but 3 goals in 8 second half minutes secured a crucial win for The Toon.

Saturday 8th February 1992
Newcastle United 3 Bristol City 0
St James' Park, Newcastle upon Tyne

It was a dream start for King Kev, and Newcastle went on to escape the drop. Looking back it was probably the most memorable of all of the Newcastle United matches I have ever attended. It was a truly magical day.

The following season, with a strengthened squad, Newcastle won the first 11 games of the campaign and never looked back, finishing as champions and gaining promotion to join the inaugural Premier League for the 1993/94 season. Keegan managed the club until 1997 during a golden era of hope and expectation that, inevitably, still ended in disappointment. Even though he signed some good defenders (Barry Venison, John Beresford and Philippe Albert for example) he had a mainly attack minded football philosophy, and he brought in some great players to achieve this. Andy Cole, Rob Lee, David Ginola, Les Ferdinand, Tino Asprilla, Alan Shearer and the returning Peter Beardsley all contributed to Newcastle United becoming known as The Entertainers during Keegan's managerial reign. Due to living in Glasgow I sadly went to very few matches at St James' Park to watch The Entertainers during these years, but Sky Sports provided live coverage of The Toon's key matches. On 4th February 1996, Newcastle were top of the Premier League with a 12 point lead over 2nd placed Manchester United. A slump in form meant they were only 4 points ahead of Manchester United when the teams met on 4th March; a game Newcastle lost 1-0 to see their lead at the top reduced to 1 point. On 3rd April, I watched the widely regarded all time greatest Premier League match where Liverpool beat Newcastle 4-3, on Sky TV in a pub in Glasgow with a Liverpool fan. This was not the happiest of nights. On 3rd May, I watched

The Toon's 1-1 draw with Nottingham Forest on Sky TV in a pub in the Lake District with some fellow Toon fans. It was 2 points dropped and a resignation that with 2 games remaining Newcastle had now blown it. We were of course left open mouthed by Keegan's legendary post match "I would love it if we beat them! Love it!" outburst towards Manchester United manager Alex Ferguson in front of the Sky TV cameras. A truly memorable moment even though we were disappointed that a Newcastle team had once again failed to deliver the success we had been craving since 1969.

WEMBLEY WOES (PART 2)

Kevin Keegan left in January 1997 and was replaced by Kenny Dalglish. Newcastle never seemed to be really in contention to win the Premier League in the 1996/97 season but results on the last day of the season saw them finish 2nd again. They qualified for the following season's UEFA Champions League memorably beating Barcelona 3-2 with a Tino Asprilla hat trick. They reached, and lost, two FA Cup Finals at the end of the 1990s. I watched the 1998 Final (lost 2-0 to Arsenal) live on TV in a pub in Dublin with friends and the 1999 Final (lost 2-0 to Manchester United) live on TV in a pub in Glasgow with friends, and whilst drowning my sorrows I felt thankful that I had not actually been at Wembley to witness these latest disappointments.

THE 21st CENTURY
FALLING IN AND OUT OF LOVE

I returned from Glasgow in 2000 to live and work in North East England again. Dave and Rob (two other long suffering Toon fans) and myself managed to secure 2 season tickets between the 3 of us for seats in the lower tier of Milburn Stand at St James' Park. There was a great view of the action from these seats in the part of the ground that very vocal fans in the Gallowgate End called The Library because everyone there generally sat in silence during the match. Dave lived in the Midlands and Rob lived in York, so because they had to travel further than me and often had family commitments on a Saturday, I invariably went to every home match, accompanied by one of them. Now in my forties, this was the first time I had ever had a season ticket. At first it was a blessing but it became a bit of a curse. With Bobby Robson as manager, Newcastle had some high Premier League finishes (4th in 2001/02 season, 3rd in 2002/03 and 5th in 2003/04) and qualified for the Champions League (a highlight was beating Juventus 1-0 in the 2002 group stage). They also reached the quarter final of 2005 UEFA Cup under then manager Graeme Souness, but as usual real success was elusive.

There were some memorable games during these seasons. On 15th September 2001, Newcastle beat Manchester United 4-3 in a thrilling encounter. The result was topped off in the last minute when Manchester United's Roy Keane received a red card after a bust up with Newcastle's Alan Shearer. Shearer scored 379 goals in his career and I was lucky enough to see a good number of these at St James' Park during his time at his hometown club. My 2 favourites were his well-controlled side footed volley from just outside the 6 yard box that flew over Peter Schmeichel and nestled in the top of the net after a perfect cross field pass from Rob Lee (versus Aston Villa on 3rd November 2001) and his powerful volley from 20 yards (versus Everton on 1st December 2002). Shearer did not have the monopoly on spectacular goals though. I saw Frenchman Laurent Robert scoring 2 great goals for The Toon in one match (versus Tottenham Hotspur on 13th December 2003) – the first a powerful left foot volley from just outside the penalty area, and the second a left foot pile driver from about 25 yards out.

By 2005, I used to regularly go drinking in Newcastle city centre after a Saturday afternoon home game with a small group of Toon supporter friends. As well as post-match analysis over a few pints, every few weeks we used to perform what we called The Pink Trick. The Football Pink (to give it its full title) was hurriedly printed on a Saturday afternoon at the Newcastle Evening Chronicle newspaper offices in the city centre. It contained match reports from that afternoon's games involving the North East's league and non-league teams, and all the results and updated tables from the English and Scottish leagues. Given the haste it was written and printed to meet a 5pm deadline, typing errors regularly occurred. A memorable one in a mid-1970s Newcastle United match report was 'Irving Nattrass tried a long-range shit'. Clearly this was a mistake (an easy one to make when the 'o' is next to the 'i' on the keyboard) and it was not describing an unspeakable act from the Toon full back. Around 5.30 pm a newspaper seller would enter the pub with his bag of Pinks (they were always printed on pink paper). Like most fans in the pub, we would buy one. One of us would then produce an old Pink from a few weeks earlier that we had kept and brought out to the match with us. We would tell the seller that he had given us two Pinks by mistake and hand him the old Pink. We would then watch as he sold this old Pink to someone else in the pub, and wait to see the reaction from the punter when the penny dropped that this was not this week's Pink he had bought. It worked every time. Little things please little minds I hear you say.

During the 2006/07 season we were all becoming gradually tired of watching the far from entertaining football at St James' Park. In November 2006, we all travelled to Germany to watch Newcastle play Eintracht Frankfurt in the UEFA Cup. We all agreed it was a great few days away apart from the 90 minutes when we had to watch the drab 0-0 draw in the fantastic Commerzbank Arena. I think the match that really epitomised how 'out of love' I was becoming with The Toon though was when they lost 4-1 at home to Portsmouth in November 2007. Pompey were 3-0 up after 11 minutes. I was not the only one feeling fed up at this match – by half time the ground was only half full (ironically I was one of the few who did stay until the end but the writing was on the wall for me).

In May 2007, Mike Ashley bought the club. A few months later I started a relationship with my now wife Anita, who is a Sunderland fan. After two seasons under Ashley's ownership, that saw Kevin Keegan return as manager for a brief stint in 2008 before an acrimonious parting, and Alan Shearer have a very short but disastrous spell as interim manager in 2009, The Toon were relegated from the Premier League at the end of the 2008/09 season.

For a number of reasons, I decided not to renew my season ticket for the 2009/10 season. First of all, I was now not really enjoying what I thought was the poor fayre being served up at St James' Park at that time; in fact it was almost becoming a fortnightly chore. Secondly, Anita had a season ticket for Sunderland, and it meant that we never met up on Saturdays when we were attending our team's home matches and socialising with others afterwards (for safe policing reasons Newcastle and Sunderland played at home on alternate Saturdays of course). She cancelled her season ticket at the same time as me. Finally, like a lot of Newcastle fans, I was not happy with the way the club was being run under Ashley's ownership - a businessman, running the club as a business and disconnected from the fans. In the 2010s, familiar themes of Ashley's tenure have been the 'on-off, club is for sale, club is not for sale' scenarios, lack of investment and selling the best players; all of which have constantly infuriated Toon fans who in the 2019/20 season boycotted home matches in their thousands. Regular fan protests now occur. There is also a regular chant at home games of "Get out of our club" aimed at Ashley. Whilst I naturally empathise with the fans chant and their undoubted allegiance to Newcastle United, the sad fact is it is not their club – it is owned by Mike Ashley. All in all, I admit I have fallen out of love a little bit with the club since 2009. Maybe it is partly an age thing? I still support them, but I do not miss going regularly to what I now feel is the general gloomy atmosphere at St James' Park, and it will stay that way until Mike Ashley sells up.

WAYNE'S WORLDIE

Gateshead began the new millennium in the Northern Premier League but at the end of the 2002/03 season they were relegated to Northern Premier League Division 1, leaving them 2 leagues away from the Conference Premier (the highest level of non-league football). The club was struggling financially at this time – a familiar trait of course – but the arrival in 2007 of new owner Graham Wood, a wealthy Gateshead-born businessman who supported the club as a youngster during their Football League years, provided renewed hope. He had made his fortune with shrewd business acumen in the USA and had now returned to the UK with the ambitious aim of returning Gateshead to the Football League.

I had been an infrequent visitor to the GIS during the first half of the decade, but in my last season as a Newcastle United season ticket holder I started going to a lot more Gateshead home games again, sometimes instead of watching The Toon on Saturdays when both teams were playing at home. Anita started coming to some Gateshead matches with me during this season. We were gradually replacing separately watching Newcastle and Sunderland with watching Gateshead together. The Heed had been promoted from the now named Unibond North Premier League the previous season via the playoffs, and were now competing in the Conference North. This was the league below the Conference Premier, and there were now two guaranteed promotion places into the Football League from the Conference Premier. Under the guidance of manager Ian Bogie (former Newcastle United, Preston North End and Port Vale midfielder) Gateshead had a fantastic season, eventually finishing in a play-off place (runners up behind Tamworth). They were the joint highest scorers in the league with 81 goals. 28 of these goals came from striker Lee Novak in 38 appearances. 'Supernovak' as he was affectionately known was sold at the end of the season to Football League One side Huddersfield Town for a North East non-league record fee at the time of £150,000. It was a joy to watch his explosive runs and clinical finishing at the GIS during the 2008/09 season. It was sad to see him leave, but together with some other good young players at this level (including James Curtis, Craig Baxter, Phil Turnbull, Wayne Phillips and Graeme Armstrong who all went on to have long careers in North East non-league football) he was part of a great young Gateshead team.

The Heed beat Southport 2-1 on aggregate in the two legged Play-off Semi-Final to set up a one match Final at the GIS against AFC Telford (Gateshead had home advantage due to their higher final league position) on Friday 8th May 2009. Anita and I were in the crowd of around 4,500 to witness Gateshead winning a close tense encounter 1-0 via an 82 minute free kick that took a slight deflection to wrong foot the Telford keeper from winger Wayne Phillips. It was not exactly a worldie from Wayne but it was without doubt one of the most memorable goals I have ever witnessed. I am not ashamed to say I had tears in my eyes when the ball hit the back of the net.

Friday 8th May 2009
Gateshead 1 AFC Telford 0
Gateshead International Stadium, Gateshead, Tyne and Wear

My hometown team, my south side of the Tyne, had achieved back-to-back promotions to the highest level of non-league football again after an 11 year absence. Before kick-off there was a rainbow over the GIS that we took as a good omen. I was prepared to believe in such things that night. (In 2020, Anita's recollection was that the rainbow appeared just after Phillips' goal. Whilst this would have been wonderfully appropriate, given that it was completely dark when the goal was scored, she eventually conceded that it happened before kick-off).

IN MILLS WE TRUST

The Heed just managed to avoid relegation in their first season in the Conference Premier, with a nail biting last day 1-0 win over AFC Wimbledon at the GIS, that Anita and I watched nervously with our friend Ken Richardson (a larger than life chap, about whom more details will be revealed in The Second Half of this book). During the next three seasons, they established a bit of a foothold in the 24 team league, finishing 14th in 2010/11, 8th in 2011/12 and 17th in 2012/13. Progress was hindered in the 2012/13 season when The Heed had to play 12 of their home games on neutral grounds due to drainage problems with the GIS pitch, making it unplayable. Anita and I attended two 'home' games at Hartlepool's Victoria Park ground in April 2013. Ian Bogie was sacked towards the end of the season. Gary Mills (who played in the Nottingham Forest team that won the 1980 European Cup) was appointed manager in September 2013. The 2013/14 season turned out to be arguably Gateshead's best ever season in non-league football.

Mills had had some previous managerial success at this level. In 2012, he led York City to a double of promotion from the Conference Premier to the Football League and an FA Trophy win at Wembley. Graham Wood appointed him hoping he could repeat the promotion achievement for Gateshead. After a poor start to the season (before Mills' appointment) the team progressed steadily up the league. After a 12 match unbeaten run in, they eventually finished 3rd in the table and faced a two-leg Play-Off Semi Final against Grimsby Town. After grinding out a 1-1 draw in the first leg at Blundell Park, a crowd of 8,202 at the GIS on Sunday 4th May 2014 watched in wonder as The Heed won the second leg 3-1 to reach Wembley for the first time in their history. Once again I had tears in my eyes at the final whistle, and it was not because of the smoke from the fireworks and flares that were being let off as hundreds of ecstatic Heed fans invaded the pitch. (I posted on Facebook at the time 'is this Gateshead or Galatasaray?'). Unlike at the Gateshead-Rochdale match in 1975 I did not invade the pitch this time – I have mellowed in my old age. After only watching Newcastle United's Wembley appearances live on TV, I resolved that this time I was going there.

GREAT EXPECTATIONS

Sunday 18th May 2014. Skrill Conference Premier Play-Off Final at Wembley Stadium. Gateshead versus Cambridge United. At stake, a place in the Football League for the winner.

The day before the Final I watched Sunderland's incredible against the odds 1973 Wembley FA Cup triumph over Leeds United on DVD. This was to help me get into a winning at Wembley mood. I had to choose Sunderland because of course sadly there have been no Newcastle United Wembley wins in my lifetime.

On Final day, I caught an early morning train to London from Newcastle Central Station (in the First Class carriage – it was a very special occasion after all). During the journey, I pondered the significance of this match. Gateshead had been unjustly voted out of the Football League 54 years earlier. Since 1968 I had supported them through thick and thin at countless matches at the GIS over the decades. Admittedly there were spells when for various reasons I had not been a regular at home games, but the club had never been far from my heart. After reading the well-produced 12 page guide called Heeding For Glory in the Sunday Sun (the North East's Sunday newspaper) on the train, I arrived in London feeling very emotional (football eh? It can do strange things to you). I was going to Wembley to watch a great little non-league club with a visionary owner, a great manager, a great group of team players and very loyal fans, try to put right a 54 year old wrong. Gateshead were now 90 minutes away from a return to the Football League, and I had a strange feeling of being both nervous and confident that they would do it. Today was the day to finish the job.

I met seven other friends at a pub in Kings Cross a few hours before kick-off – a mix of Gateshead born and bred lads who I used to go to Heed matches with in the 1970s and 1980s (including my brother Kevin who had travelled from

Liverpool) and some Newcastle United supporter mates who had jumped on the bandwagon to support The Heed on what was hopefully to be a big day (they were most welcome of course). After 5 pints in the glorious sunshine, we travelled via the Underground to Wembley Stadium, where we met my uncle. This is my uncle who, with my late grandfather, took me to my first football match at Redheugh Park in 1968. Now 73 years old, he was at Gateshead's final match in the Football League in 1960. I thought how fitting it would be if he was at the match where they seal a return to it. Walking up to Wembley, we were stopped by Jeff Brown, the sports reporter for BBC Look North, and his cameraman. Jeff held one of those big furry sausage type microphones near to me and asked how I was feeling about today's game. I had no problem telling him. Given I was loaded with alcohol, I was surprised to find my 15 seconds of emotional outpourings made the cut on that evening's Look North local news programme.

WEMBLEY WOES (PART 3)

After all of this pre-match fervour, it was perhaps with some degree of inevitability that it ended in disappointment. Gateshead gave it a good go but they lost.

Sunday 18th May 2014
Gateshead 1 Cambridge United 2
Wembley Stadium, London

After their great winning streak leading up to this match it sadly proved to be the day that the team did not maintain that momentum. Some players did not quite play at their best, and The Heed were undone by conceding 2 second half goals from set pieces – a corner and a free kick. Once Cambridge took that 2 goal lead, it was always going to be a tall order but a late Jack Lester goal for The Heed gave a bit of hope. Gateshead legend James Curtis (he made 596 appearances for the club between 2003 and 2016) agonisingly headed just wide during injury time. If he had scored I seriously think Gateshead would have gone on to win the match during extra time because they had suddenly started to play better towards the end of the second half and Cambridge looked to be tiring. It was not to be though. It had been an incredible season and we had a great day out watching The Heed's first ever Wembley appearance, but my 100 Years of Hurt continued with another failure to clear the final hurdle.

On 3rd January 2015 another milestone was reached when Gateshead played in the 3rd Round of the FA Cup for the first time in 60 years – and therefore the first time in my lifetime. Anita and I travelled to the Hawthorns for the tie with West Bromwich Albion, who were struggling in the relegation zone of the Premier League at that time. They had appointed Tony Pulis as manager the week before and he chose to sit in the stand for his first match in charge. However, the Gateshead underdogs started well and were more than holding their own for the first half hour of the match, prompting Pulis to leave his comfy seat and move down to the dugout to start shouting at the Albion players to buck their ideas up. After a good performance for the first 40 minutes, Gateshead conceded 2 goals just before half time which dampened our mood a bit. The difference in class showed in the second half but the large travelling Heed Army never gave up singing. When 4-0 down they were singing 'We're going to win 5-4' and when Albion then scored a fifth goal they carried on singing the same chant but changed the words to 'We're going to win 6-5'. The final score was 7-0.

In the five seasons that followed, Gateshead remained in the top tier of non-league football but never made the Play-Offs again. In complete contrast to the fantastic 2013/14 season, the 2018/19 season was one of complete turmoil (further details of this in The Second Half of this book).

WILL THE HURT EVER END?

I often ask myself will Newcastle or Gateshead ever win anything significant again in my lifetime. The usual answer is no, but football is 'a funny old game'. Against all the odds Denmark (1992) and Greece (2004) won the UEFA European Championship, and 5,000-1 outsiders Leicester City pulled off one of the greatest sporting shocks ever when they won the Premier League title in the 2015/16 season. I live in hope - but there is also the old saying 'It's the hope that kills you'.

CHAPTER

TALES FROM WEARSIDE

TYNE AND WEIRDO

November 1977. My first day at work in my first ever job. As a shy 16-year-old, I joined my new workmates at the 11 am tea break. One lad, who was a Sunderland fan, asked me where I lived.

"Gateshead" I replied.

"Ah, so do you support Sunderland?"

"No, I support Newcastle…but I go to watch Gateshead as well"

"I would have thought with you living south of the Tyne you would support Sunderland".

"No, but I don't dislike Sunderland". I then added something that I had always thought, but I am pretty sure that I had never said out loud to anyone at any time, until now, "I like to see all of the North East teams do well".

My last comment was met with total disbelief by both Newcastle and Sunderland supporting colleagues sitting around the table. The two cities are in the same County - Tyne and Wear - but to suggest that I wanted to see both football teams do well branded me as a weirdo – a 'Tyne and Weirdo'. The rivalry between Newcastle fans and Sunderland fans is, of course, just one of hundreds of similar local rivalries all over the footballing world. Both clubs have large loyal followings, and unquestionably Sunderland fans are equally as passionate about their team as Newcastle fans are about theirs. The level of antagonism between the two sets of fans ranges from good natured banter to pathological hatred. I have personally always been at the friendly banter end of this spectrum with Sunderland fans, and I can trace the origin of my impartiality towards the club to the 1973 FA

Cup Final. Sunderland, then in the Second Division, faced First Division Leeds United, one of the best teams in England at the time. I was by this time a 12 year old Newcastle United and Gateshead fan, but my cousin and one of my friends supported Sunderland, and it felt right to me to join them in supporting a North East of England team in the Cup Final. With a red and white scarf draped over my parents' recently acquired colour television, we watched Sunderland upset all of the odds and beat Leeds 1-0, thanks to a 32nd minute goal from Ian Porterfield and an incredible double save by Sunderland goalkeeper Jimmy Montgomery midway through the second half (it is worth checking YouTube footage of this if you are not familiar with it).

Saturday 5th May 1973
Sunderland 1 Leeds United 0
BBC Television (Live from Wembley Stadium, London)

It was a remarkable achievement and I celebrated it. As an impressionable youngster, this was undoubtedly the day that I decided "I like to see all of the North East teams do well". I did not feel then, and have never felt since, the same intense rivalry that my Newcastle supporter friends have towards Sunderland. It often seems like I am a lone voice – I must certainly be in the minority – but this is my long-held view.

In the 1970s, Derek 'Dekka' Muse (a friend who accompanied me on some groundhopping trips detailed in The Second Half of this book) used to go the St James' Park one Saturday afternoon to watch Newcastle and then Roker Park the following Saturday afternoon to watch Sunderland (he now has a season ticket for Sunderland only). This was quite common in the 1950s, 1960s and 1970s, when working men in particular just wanted to enjoy some live football in their locality on a Saturday after the harshness of the working week. With the rise of more organised football hooliganism during the 1970s, local rivalries between clubs including Newcastle and Sunderland seemed to intensify and have continued ever since. I seriously doubt there is anyone in 2020 who goes to watch both clubs' home games on alternate Saturdays.

(SOL)IDARITY WITH ANITA

As I recounted in Chapter 3, my wife Anita and I proved that love can conquer the great divide between Newcastle and Sunderland fans. However, like many others she cannot understand my "I like to see all of the North East teams do well" viewpoint. There are a lot of teams she likes to see do well though – namely Sunderland and any team that is playing against Newcastle. Our general good natured banter does not of course extend to Tyne-Wear derby days. Whilst I have never wished any ill on Sunderland FC, I naturally want them to lose when they play Newcastle in the Tyne-Wear derby. I have been to a number of these derbies at St James' Park over the years and I do not enjoy the usually toxic atmosphere at them. The derby match I particularly did not enjoy was in November 2000 when Sunderland's keeper Thomas Sorensen saved the normally totally reliable penalty taker Alan Shearer's spot kick and Sunderland won 2-1. Thankfully I have avoided being caught up amongst any of the fighting that sadly sometimes accompanies the football. I have never been to a Tyne-Wear derby when Sunderland are the home team and, at this stage in my life, I think I will now give up on ever having that potentially risky experience.

There have only been a handful of occasions when I have journeyed to Wearside to watch a Sunderland home game over the years. The first time was the one and only time I went to a match at their now demolished Roker Park ground. To be more accurate, it was actually to watch Sunderland Reserves in a pre-season friendly against Nissan Reserves from Japan. It was a 7.30 pm kick off on Wednesday 25 July 1984, the first XIs of both teams having met also at Roker Park four days earlier. The large Nissan car manufacturing plant opened in Sunderland later in the same year. The match was certainly not the most appealing proposition but a friend and I had been invited by a local business into the hospitality area, so we figured that some complimentary pre-match food and drink would make up for the 90 minute tame kick around that would surely follow. This proved to be correct because I have absolutely no recollection of what happened in this match. (Although I prefer to watch football on the terraces, I have been lucky enough to be invited to watch many games in hospitality, mainly at St James Park but also at Glasgow Celtic, Glasgow Rangers, Hampden Park and Partick Thistle. I have enjoyed hospitality at other sports too; rugby union internationals at Murrayfield and club matches at Newcastle Falcons, cricket at Riverside (Durham County Cricket Club), and golf at St Andrews and Loch Lomond. The invitations were invariably from business connections, which I very rarely turned down, prompting my wife to rather harshly call me a corporate whore. Unlike this Sunderland Reserves match at Roker Park, I usually thoroughly enjoyed the sporting action as well as the free lunch).

Sunderland left Roker Park and moved to the purpose-built all-seater 42,000 capacity Stadium of Light (The SOL) in July 1997. Almost a decade later I attended a match there. A Sunderland supporting friend had a ticket going spare so I agreed to go to The SOL with him on the proviso that he did not let it slip that I was a Newcastle fan. The date was Saturday 24th February 2007. Sunderland's opponents were Derby County. Both teams were doing well in the Championship (Second Level of English Football) and both went on to win promotion to the Premier League at the end of the season. Sunderland's manager was the enigmatic Roy Keane ('Keano'). After running the gauntlet in a pub full of fans wearing red and white striped shirts in Sunderland city centre prior to kick-off, I remained quiet when David Connolly gave Sunderland a first half lead from the penalty spot. We were in the stand opposite the dugouts and I could see that Keano, directly opposite us and looking very stylish in what would very likely be a very expensive suit, showed no emotion at all at the goal. Derby's Giles Barnes equalised on the hour mark, slotting the ball home after a mazy dribble through the Sunderland defence. It really was a great goal but when I said this to the fans around me they did not seem to agree, so I decided to revert back to watching the match in silence (safety first). With the match heading for a draw, an injury time winner from Sunderland's Liam Miller sent The SOL into raptures. The only people not celebrating wildly were the Derby fans housed behind one of the goals, myself….and the enigmatic bloke in the very expensive suit standing with his arms folded in front of the dugouts.

After living to tell the tale following that first visit to The SOL, I went four more times and never seen Sunderland win again. Anita and my Sunderland supporter friends are naturally calling me a jinx, but my Newcastle supporter friends are suddenly encouraging me to follow my "I like to see all of the North East teams do well" philosophy and go to The SOL more often. One of the four defeats was against Arsenal on Saturday 11th February 2012 when Anita and I witnessed the great Thierry Henry's stoppage time winner – his last ever goal in English football. On Saturday 29th July 2017 we saw Celtic (who had 9,000 fans in the away end) thrash Sunderland 5-0 in a pre-season friendly. It was new Sunderland manager Simon Grayson's first home match in charge, but when I went to the toilet at half time there were Sunderland fans in there incredibly already wanting him to be sacked. He was eventually given the boot in October 2017 after a disastrous start to the season; a season that ended with Sunderland being relegated from the Championship to League One.

On the subject of half time toilet banter, I recall going into the packed gents toilets in the Milburn Stand at St James Park during half time at a particular match. Picture the usual scenario of a dozen or so fans relieving themselves at the urinals and another 3 dozen or so fans queueing behind them. The whole toilet is suddenly chanting 'Lewis! Lewis!' over and over again. The North East born and bred actor Kevin Whately was one of those standing at the urinal – he played Sergeant Lewis in the popular TV series Inspector Morse. Very sportingly he just laughed and said 'For God's sake, can a bloke not have a piss in peace?', and everyone cheered.

Given that my Tyne and Weirdo empathy for Sunderland is inexcusable behaviour in the eyes of Newcastle fans, I feel it is only fitting to redeem myself a little and end this Chapter with some banter at Sunderland's expense, so here goes....the best performance I have ever seen at The SOL was on Thursday 21st June 2012 by Bruce Springsteen and the E Street Band.

CHAPTER

A WEE BIT O' SCOTTISH FITBA'

In 1992 I left the North East of England to live and work in Glasgow for what turned out to be the rest of the decade. It was a good move for my banking career (and I had two further promotions during my time in Scotland) but the extra work responsibility made finding the time to regularly watch football more difficult. The 300 mile round trip from Glasgow to Newcastle or Gateshead meant I was unable to watch my two sides of the Tyne very often in the 1990s, but I had some memorable matchday experiences in the football mad city of Glasgow to compensate for this.

PUNCHED BY A RANGERS FAN

As a youngster my Scottish team was always Glasgow Celtic. I think it started when the junior school football team I played for aged 11 wore the green and white hooped shirts of the Celts. I was of course aware of the rivalry between Celtic and Glasgow Rangers (The Old Firm), but I did not fully appreciate how intense that rivalry was for some fans, and the magnitude of the religious sectarianism behind it all, until I lived there amongst it. I was honesty quite shocked when my new boss at work told me that it was important to understand that there could be occasions where it might not be advisable to say I supported Celtic. I quickly learnt the rules. When someone asked me what team I supported, sometimes it was safer to say Newcastle United (this was of course actually true). If they then asked what Glasgow team I liked the best, it was advisable not to take the 50-50 chance of saying either Celtic or Rangers with some people - the safest answer was often Partick Thistle. When finding out I was called Michael, some people would say "I assume you're a Catholic" and immediately pigeonhole me (for the record, I am a Catholic). I found this behaviour a bit disconcerting at first but I soon got used to it, and, of course, it was only from a small minority. I made some lifelong friends during my time in Glasgow, on both sides of the religious divide, who did not care at all about what school I went to. On one occasion, I was chatting with a Rangers fan at a hospitality event for Glasgow business connections. After some initial good natured Celtic-Rangers banter, he became decidedly more drunk and aggressive, and suddenly threw a punch at me. He was restrained by other business colleagues and bundled away. Apart from this, I was never on the receiving end of 'a Glasgow Kiss' or any other form of violence during my time in the wonderful city of Glasgow and the beautiful country of Scotland.

THE JUNGLE

My first visit to the Celtic's Parkhead stadium was on 18th December 1993 for their match against Hibernian. The club was experiencing major financial difficulties at that time and attendances had dropped significantly due to poor performances. For safety reasons, The Jungle – the legendary standing only concrete terracing opposite the Main Stand – was due to be knocked down (this was eventually carried out in the summer of 1994), together with the large terraces behind each goal. They were all to be replaced by seated areas. My Celtic supporting friend James thought it would be a good idea that I watched a match in The Jungle before it was demolished. It could hold around 8,000 fans, and could rival the charged atmosphere of Liverpool's Kop stand when full of the green and white hooped shirt wearing, sectarian song singing, Irish flag waving Celtic fans. The Jungle was sadly only half full on this cold Saturday afternoon in December 1993, so James and I did not experience the full crushing effect. Similar to what I had witnessed at Newcastle United in the early 1990s, a large fans' pressure group called Celts For Change were in another part of the ground with 'Sack the Board, Back The Team' banners (their protests were successful when, in March 1994, businessman Fergus McCann acquired a controlling share of the club from the family dynasties that had owned it for over 100 years).

Saturday 18th December 1993
Celtic 1 Hibernian 0
Parkhead, Glasgow

The off the field activity was definitely more entertaining than what was being served up to us on the field – Celtic winning a drab encounter 1-0. The Jungle had witnessed some classic matches over the years including some great Old Firm encounters and European Cup ties, but I was still very pleased to have stood in it once for this poor one.

A FAMILIAR FEELING

I was in a different country watching a different team but the feeling of disappointment watching Celtic during the 1990s was all too familiar to watching Newcastle and Gateshead. Fergus McCann saved the club from bankruptcy, injected cash to put it onto a steady footing and oversaw the redevelopment of Parkhead into an impressive 60,000 capacity all seated stadium. In 1996 I was invited into the Hospitality Suite for a match at Parkhead by a Celtic supporting mortgage broker contact. After some food and drink, I was disappointed to find we were now heading outside into the cold Glaswegian winter rather staying inside in the warmth and watching through a big glass window as is the general norm in football club hospitality areas. I soon cheered up though when I discovered that my very comfortable green leather seat was heated, and I could watch the match in pleasant surroundings (apart from the man in the row behind us with a bit of a downer on Celtic's central defender Peter Grant, who criticised him – unjustly - every time he touched the ball).

Celtic have a large fan base and there was no shortage of Celtic supporting friends from Scotland to attend matches with. There was also a contingent of North East of England based fans who travelled up regularly to Parkhead. A few pre-match pints were usually consumed in Baird's Bar on Glasgow's Gallowgate. This was very much a Celtic pub with green and white décor, Celtic flags and photos everywhere, and the whole of the 1967 European Cup Final being shown on the televisions in the bar on a constant loop. This was of course arguably Celtic's greatest triumph when the Lisbon Lions beat Inter Milan 2-1 to become the first British club to win European football's top prize. The Celtic team were all born within 30 miles of Glasgow (in fact most were born within 10 miles) so it was very much a team of local lads winning the European Cup – a feat that will surely never be repeated by any team in the modern game.

On some Saturdays I took the car and parked it with dozens of others on the road next to the ground. There were no formal Council parking charges here but local youngsters would corner you as soon as you got out of your car to "watch it for you mister" while you were at the match. It was always safer to just agree a price and let them watch it for you. I do not know whether they stayed beside my car constantly during the match, or whether they went elsewhere and just came back at quarter to five, but they were always true to their word as guardians of the vehicle. I recall one match where after a long post-match discussion just outside the ground, I returned to find my car was the only one still parked on the road. The young lad who said he would watch it for me was still there, playing keepy-up with his Celtic-branded football, next to my car. I was truly amazed and gave him a bonus payment for his overtime shift.

I enjoyed watching some good players during this time, including Paola Di Canio, Pierre van Hooijdonk, Jorge Cadete, John Collins, Paul McStay and my favourite Celtic player of all at that time Henrik Larsson, but they were struggling to compete with The Auld Enemy Rangers, who won the league title 9 seasons in a row from 1988/89 to 1996/97 inclusive (equalling Celtic's own 9 seasons in a row of league title wins in the late 1960s and early 1970s). A Celtic win on the last day of the 1997/98 season denied Rangers their 10 in a row, and provided me with a rare celebration in my North of the Border Years of Hurt.

THE JAGS

In 1995 another hospitality invite from a firm of Glasgow Surveyors resulted in me forming a soft spot for Partick Thistle, which has endured to this day. Many Partick fans will tell you that endured is the most apt word to use to describe supporting the boys in yellow, black and red – commonly known as The Jags. They have not had too much to shout since their formation in 1876 (they won the Scottish Cup in 1921 and Scottish League Cup in 1972 – and that's it for major honours).

On the cold Tuesday evening of 7th March 1995, the hospitality at their Firhill ground for a Scottish Premier Division match against Dundee United was excellent. I was especially impressed by their Chairman who hosted the hospitality with self-depreciating humour about Partick's paucity of success during its 100 years plus history. Among the old classics he trotted out, like a stand-up comedian in a social club, were "Some people think the full name of this club is Partick Thistle Nil" and "I will show you all around the Trophy Room now, that won't take long". He also told the Glaswegian equivalent of The Fergie Time joke ("Rangers scored a 97th minute equaliser against us and I asked the referee to justify where the 7 minutes additional time came from. He agreed it was a lot and he was worried that Rangers were never going to score"). The match was a typical relegation tussle, but at the final whistle the full name of the club tonight was Partick Thistle Two – and it was Dundee United Nil. The Jags secured 3 valuable points in the relegation fight. (Partick avoided relegation at the end of the season and Dundee United were relegated).

Four days later I went to Firhill again with a friend for Partick's match against Aberdeen. This time I stood on the open terracing behind one of the goals. It was a sunny Saturday afternoon, the crowd was over 6,000 (a large contingent of Aberdeen fans had travelled to Glasgow) and it was an exciting 2-2 draw (Aberdeen full back Stephen Wright scored one of the best goals I have ever witnessed – a looping shot from the halfway line).

Saturday 11th March 1995
Partick Thistle 2 Aberdeen 2
Firhill Stadium, Glasgow

I really enjoyed being amongst The Jags' fans who were, by and large, a very friendly bunch untainted by any Old Firm sectarianism. Partick prides itself on being a family club and, after watching them twice during this week, I developed a lifelong attachment. I have watched them many times since, even though they generally only add to my North of The Border Years of Hurt.

JOINING THE ARMY

I was born in England and I am a patriot. I can in no way ever be described as being anti-English. However, I have bizarrely never fully felt the fervour of supporting the England national football team over the Scotland national team. I suspect it is partly because I have Scottish ancestry on my mother's side of the family tree. Also, being born and bred in the North East of England, means I have always lived closer to Hampden Park, Glasgow (Scotland's national stadium) than Wembley, London (England's national stadium). In the football sense, I feel a strange affinity to Scotland before England. This has obviously only added to my Years of Hurt. That said, I never went to Hampden until I lived in Glasgow. The first time I did was for a friendly warm up match against Australia in March 1996, ahead of Scotland's participation in the UEFA European Championship in June (Euro '96). It was great to visit the national stadium at last but I am struggling to remember anything in particular about the game (the record books show it was a 1-0 Scotland victory with a goal from Ally McCoist). Scotland were knocked out in the group stages of the Euro '96 tournament, which was held in England. They were defeated 2-0 by England at Wembley in one of their 3 group matches. The second England goal was a classic from Gateshead-born Paul Gascoigne (check YouTube if you are not familiar with the genius of it). The only other match I saw at Hampden was on Saturday 23rd November 1996 when the oldest club in Scottish football Queen's Park FC (who at that time owned Hampden Park and leased it to the Scottish Football Association for Scotland's international matches and domestic Cup Finals) lost 2-3 to Inverness Caledonian Thistle in a Third Division match. Some friends and I paid slightly more than the general admission charge to also have a very interesting behind the scenes pre-match stadium tour that day.

The next time I watched Scotland was on Tuesday 2nd April 1997 at Parkhead for their crucial World Cup Qualifier against Austria. I was in the 43,295 crowd with a few Scottish friends. The atmosphere was electric. The legendary Tartan Army (who my friends had made me an honorary member of) were out in force, with saltire painted faces, waving flags and singing non-stop during the match. They basically sang three songs on constant rotation throughout. Firstly, one to the tune of 'Que Sera Sera' rhyming 'whatever will be' with 'going to gay Paree' (the 1998 World Cup Finals were held in France). Secondly, a chant of 'Stand up if you hate the English' (I could be wrong but it certainly seemed that I was the only Englishman in the stadium so to stay safe I stood up with the partisan crowd). Finally, their famous and totally non PC chant about Jimmy Hill (the late football pundit/presenter who described a great goal by Scotland's David Narey against Brazil in the 1982 World Cup Finals as a toe poke. The Tartan Army have never forgiven him for that comment). I was fortunate to witness one of the most glorious nights for the Scottish national team (there have not been too many of them).

Tuesday 27th April 1997
Scotland 2 Austria 0
Parkhead, Glasgow

Scotland won 2-0 with two goals from Kevin Gallacher (who went on to play for Newcastle in 1999). I had a perfect view of his 78th minute second goal – a glorious drive from the edge of the penalty area into the far top corner of the net. The crowd erupted when it went in, knowing that this important win put them in a great position to qualify for France '98. They clinched qualification in October 1997 finishing 2nd in the group behind Austria.

THE TOON AT IBROX

It would be fair to say that "I do not like to see all of the Glasgow teams do well" but that did not stop me from going to watch Rangers on a few occasions. Their 50,000 all seater Ibrox Stadium is very impressive. I was invited to hospitality there twice and it was excellent (it pains me to say it was better than Celtic's).

The first time I went to a match at Ibrox though, Rangers were not playing. It was for the 1994 Scottish Junior Cup Final between Largs Thistle and Glenafton Athletic. Lest anyone thinks Junior football in Scotland is played by schoolboys and girls, I would clarify that it is played by grown men and is akin to lower level non-league football in England. I had a few friends in Glasgow who were originally from the beautiful seaside town of Largs in North Ayrshire about 30 miles south west of Glasgow. Largs Thistle were in their first ever Junior Cup Final and were the clear underdogs, but they triumphed 1-0 in front of an 8,668 crowd. My Largs' friends and I had a memorable celebration in the pubs of Glasgow's Southside that evening.

Sunday 15th May 1994
Largs Thistle 1 Glenafton Athletic 0
Ibrox Stadium, Glasgow

My next visit to Ibrox was with some Newcastle United supporting friends who came to Glasgow from the North East for a 4 team pre-season tournament. On Friday 5th August 1994 we watched Sampdoria beat Rangers, followed by The Toon beating Manchester United on penalties. The following day we watched Rangers beat Manchester United in the 3rd place play-off match (most memorable moment was Eric Cantona being booed by the entire stadium after being sent off for a very bad tackle), then watched Newcastle lose (inevitably) 3-1 to Sampdoria in the Final.

On Wednesday 1st November 1995, I watched Rangers being totally outclassed by, and losing 4-0 to, Italian giants Juventus in a UEFA Champions League game. The Juve team included Del Piero and Vialli, and it was a joy to watch their perfect tactical passing game. I recall my friends and I made a particularly quick exit from Ibrox when the match finished though, to avoid the missiles being thrown down by the away fans who were in the seats above us. It appeared that there were some Glaswegians of good Italian Catholic extraction amongst the Juve fans, showing their affinity to Celtic. It soon calmed down though. This was the closest I have ever been, or ever want to be, to Old Firm trouble.

CHAPTER

DEEPDALE (AND WHAT I LAUGHINGLY CALL MY PLAYING CAREER)

TEENAGE DREAMS

Anyone who started to enjoy watching football from an early age would likely have had dreams of becoming a professional footballer one day. I certainly did. Unfortunately, like countless other dreamers, I soon discovered I did not have enough skill and ability to make the grade. It was not for the want of practice though. From the age of nine and into my mid-teenage years, I would play football at every opportunity, usually for hours on end. This could be in the front street or back lane of my Gateshead home (jumpers, street lamps or garage doors for goalposts), or in the nearby Saltwell Park (where my friends and I could play freely on a large grassed area - like Wembley but with a bit of dog poo to watch out for here and there). In the back lane we would play games like Doors (where each player had someone's wooden back door to defend. You would be 'out' if you let 3 goals in or, as was generally more likely, the home owner of the door you were defending came out to complain about the ball being kicked at it) and Spotkick (where players took it in turns to kick the ball against a brick wall. If your shot missed the wall you lost a life. You had 8 lives i.e. the letters of S,P,O,T,K,I,C,K.).

In Saltwell Park, there was often enough lads wanting to play to have 11-a-side, even 12 or 13-a –side matches, which could last for hours, well over the standard 90 minutes, with final scores like 15-14. In this example, at 14-14 it could have been mutually agreed that the next goal scored is the winner, so that we could at least have a short break to go home and eat some food. However, there was a bizarre rule that, when the next goal scored is the winner was agreed by both (hungry) teams, a team losing 15-0 could still claim victory if they scored the next goal. One lad who also lived close to Saltwell Park and played with us sometimes was

Neil Aspin (who went on to play over 600 times in the Football League, mainly for Leeds United and Port Vale). To my knowledge no one else from this group played football at any decent level. One lad, who was not blessed with a lot of footballing skill, often had the novel idea of taking a fallen branch from a tree, spearing a piece of dog poo on one end of it, and brandishing it during a game. Calling it The Shit Stick he would stand in central defence and lunge at opponents with it. It was a highly effective deterrent – I doubt even Christiano Ronaldo could dribble around a defender armed with a Shit Stick.

We all loved playing football back then but there was extremely limited scope for us to develop. I was considered to be a useful central defender during my schooldays, but sadly not outstanding enough to benefit from the additional coaching that a very limited number of fellow schoolboys received to improve and develop their skills. Nowadays there are much more opportunities for boys and girls in that same age group, including formal teams to play for in competitive leagues, and a greater number of qualified coaches to nurture individual talent. I am in no way bitter about this though. I have friends with teenage children who are reaping the benefit of it all, and I regularly encourage them to follow their dream.

CHAMPIONS OF GATESHEAD

I may not have had the football career I dreamt about in those adolescent years, but I have still had some memorable moments playing football. During May 1972, I won two medals as part of a great junior school team. Playing at centre-half, we won the Gateshead West League at a canter and then went on to win the Gateshead Teachers' Association Cup (that was a kind of Super Cup Final between the West and East League winners). This was the only time that I ever had the unbridled pleasure of doing a lap of honour, as I ran around the pitch parading the trophy with my teammates to the (albeit very sparse) crowd. The Final was also unique in that it was the only time my dad came to watch me playing competitive schools football. Our coach/teacher said to him during the match that I was having a really good game, and my dad, in full no understanding of the game of football mode, replied that he was pleased to hear that because he had no idea whether I was or not!

THE BACK ELEVEN

Four months later I left junior school and started at secondary grammar school in Newcastle. I could not secure a place in the school football team due to stiff competition for places. I had to settle for just playing for the house team each year (there were six houses who competed in various sports each term). One house football match sticks firmly in the memory. In 1974, my house team were playing against the best team in the house league. The match drew quite a crowd of fellow pupils because it was expected that we would be hammered. We desperately wanted to prove them all wrong, and decided to play very defensive tactics for the whole 40 minutes that these matches lasted. Not for us A Back Four – for this game we adopted A Back Eleven. The whole team parked in our penalty area, defending wave upon wave of attacks, crosses into the box, and corner after corner. I remember heading the ball off the goal line in the later stages of the game when our keeper was beaten. We held out for a goalless draw and celebrated it like a win in front of the stunned crowd.

THE RINGER

In 1986 I was part of 5 a side team that emphatically won a 12 team league at the Newcastle University Sports Centre. To be honest I was very definitely the fifth best player in this team who won 10 and drew 1 of their 11 games but I played my part and I have still got the medal to prove it. In the same year, a friend of mine (Dave) asked me if I would at short notice play in an 11 a side league match for his works team in Spennymoor, County Durham who were a man short. I agreed and, because I was not registered to play for them in this league, I had to pretend to be someone who was. I played as a ringer left winger and had quite a lonely time out on the wing because bizarrely no one would pass to me, or even speak to me, apart from Dave. With about ten minutes to go and the match still goalless, I got a rare touch of the ball and ran down the left wing with it to the edge of penalty box. Two attackers in the box were screaming for the ball so I put in what I thought was a pretty decent cross. The cross cleared the defenders, and the attackers, and the goalkeeper, and ended up in the back of the net. I waited in vain to be congratulated by anyone other than Dave, even though I had scored what turned out to be the winning goal for them under a pseudonym. The Ringer never played for them again.

PLAYING AT DEEPDALE

In 1994 I had the great pleasure, for the one and only time, of playing 11 a side football at a Football League ground. It was at Preston North End's Deepdale stadium, which, given that Preston were established in 1880, is the oldest ground in terms of continuous use by a Football League team. They were in the Third Division (today's League One) at that time and played on an artificial pitch, which they rented out to local teams to generate extra income. Hence the bank I worked for hired the pitch and I played for a Branches team versus Head Office XI. I played right back and we won 5-1 (the goal conceded was not my fault of course). It felt fantastic playing in a proper stadium, even though it was almost empty (attendance was 30 rough head count). After the match and the communal bath, three of us continued to behave like some proper footballers do, by going to a Preston nightclub and drinking until the early hours.

A year later, I was capped for Scotland. It was another 11 a side match organised within the bank I worked at. This time staff from Scotland played staff from (mainly Northern) England. Based more on the fact that I had lived and worked in Glasgow for three years at this point rather than being due to my Scottish ancestry, I was enticed to desert my country of birth and play for Scotland. After a tight goalless first half, the boys from North of the Border took control and with 10 minutes to go led 3-1. I was playing as an overlapping right winger, was starting to flag a bit and hoping to see the game out without any further exertion. Our captain had other ideas though and, with the English lads pushing up to try to salvage something from the match, passed the ball to me on the halfway line shouting something like "come on Stouty, take it down the wing". I had acres of space, and ran down the wing unhindered and into the penalty area. I rounded a defender and fired the ball towards the goal. I did not think the shot was hard enough to trouble the keeper but as he went down to save it the ball bobbled in the barren goalmouth and went past him. It just crept over the goal line but they all count. I had scored for Scotland in a 4-1 win over England and it felt good.

THE TWILIGHT YEARS

On returning to the North East at the start of the 21st Century, I was almost 40 years old and I decided that my days of playing 11 a side football were over. It would be 5 a side only from now on, and where possible against players in the same age group. Inevitably though, I would sometimes be playing against much younger lads in their twenties. This was true in 2003 when I played for a team in a 5 a side league at the Newcastle University Sports Centre (I have a 1986 champions' medal from that league you will recall). In contrast, this 2003 team was one of the worst in the league. We lost every week, sometimes heavily, and by Week 6 everyone was despondent. Some lads were not only going for a few post-match pints, they were having a pint before the match. On Week 7 we were up against the only other team in the league who had lost all their games; this was the proverbial wooden spoon match. I was determined we would win this match to restore some pride. I made sure no one had a pre-match pint and introduced some tactics. We managed to grind out a 5-4 victory. We went to the pub, I bought them all a pint and told them I can no longer keep pace with all these young 'uns, so this was my last competitive match in what I lovingly but laughably call my football career.

I continued to play more friendly 5 a side games on both indoor and outdoor pitches in the Newcastle area, generally with work colleagues in the same age group. When I reached my fifties, I hung my trainers up completely; it was watching football only from now on for me.

CHAPTER

WORLD IN EMOTION (FOR ONE MONTH ONLY)

WE LOVE YOU HARRY !!!!!!

Picture the scene in Anytown, Randomshire, England.

11th July 2018. The semi-final of the World Cup. England versus Croatia.

In the outdoor 'World Cup Zone' there are beer and food tents and a very big screen to watch the footy. The sun is shining and expectations are high. Four young ladies who have clearly modelled their look on the girl band Little Mix cheer every time Harry Kane touches the ball. They normally don't like football but this is the World Cup! The Harry they normally love is Harry Styles from the boy band One Direction, but for the last few weeks they have been caught up in the euphoria of the World Cup so they all love Harry Kane instead. In fact, one of them has started to like the other Harry in the squad - Harry McGuire - and she would switch allegiance to him if only his head wasn't so large.

There are groups of lads drinking lager and cider. They certainly do like football. They've got 3 Lions on their shirts and 3 pints on the go (there's massive queues at the beer tent so it makes sense to buy a triple round). Some of them have also got 3 tattoos on their arms and/or legs (England badge, domestic team badge, and either mum or name of wife/girlfriend). Some lads are wearing waistcoats, sales of which have increased dramatically since England manager Gareth Southgate has been sporting one with style during the tournament.

Suddenly there are wild celebrations as England score early on. Plastic pints of lager are thrown into the air, soaking everyone who are hoping it is JUST lager. Despair later as Croatia score twice to end England's World Cup dream for another four years – that recurring broken dream that has been ongoing since 1966.

It's over. The young ladies can go back to following Little Mix instead. The lads can put their Gareth waistcoats back into the wardrobe, never to be worn again.... unless....2022 World Cup Final??....you've got to have a dream....

THE FOUR-YEAR ITCH

It is widely accepted that football is the most popular spectator sport in both the UK and the world. Not everyone likes it of course, but every four years an event takes place when it feels like everyone in the world is interested in watching football (at least for a short time) - the Finals of the FIFA World Cup. It is often called The Greatest Show on Earth and it is hard to argue with that. It is certainly the greatest sporting event in terms of having the biggest worldwide television audience and being the most expensive to host. If England is anything to go by during a World Cup summer (and I am pretty sure it is typical of most countries in the world), people who are not normally football fans are extremely likely to be drawn like a magnet to watch it – particularly if England have qualified for the Finals (in my lifetime they usually have but sometimes they don't of course). Painting your face with the St George's Cross or putting England flags on top of your car are optional, but you will very likely be caught up in the feeling of national pride for a month or so (if England reach the Final) or until they are knocked out – whichever is the sooner. Wherever it is held, I love the overall spectacle of the tournament and the camaraderie between fans from different countries. It is where the world's best footballers play on the world's biggest stage for the greatest prize – and it generally never fails to deliver.

As a football fan of course I have never needed any encouragement to completely immerse myself in the World Cup. I have never been lucky enough or, given the huge expense, realistically rich enough to go to a World Cup tournament. I have been restricted to watching it from the sofa at home or in pubs in the UK and bars abroad.

Just as the players aim to be in peak condition for the tournament, meticulous preparation is also important for sofa based fans to guarantee maximum enjoyment. A good supply of food and drink is a given, and you need to, if possible, book time off when an important unmissable match is live on the TV when you should be at work. I personally always need to have a World Cup wallchart (normally a free one from a Sunday newspaper – scores must be filled in promptly without fail after every match). Panini Sticker Books used to be a thing for me (they were usually never completed) but I have gradually grown out of that phase. You also need to select the players for your World Cup Fantasy Football team, place your bets on who will win etc., and you will no doubt be asked sometime somewhere to pay £5 and pick a team out of the hat in a sweepstake ("Come on, have a go, it's only a fiver, there's a good chance you will pick the winner, there's only 3 teams left and one of them is Brazil". You hand over your £5 and pick out Honduras). From the 2010 tournament, Anita introduced an additional requirement of putting up bunting at the front of the house with the flags of the competing nations on it. Well, it's only once every four years, you might as well make a special effort.

Given my desire to see all of the North East teams do well, it is perhaps no surprise to know that I also like to see all of the Home Nations do well. That is England, Scotland and Ireland (Northern and Republic of). I have omitted Wales because up to and including 2018, they have never qualified for the World Cup Finals during my lifetime.

When Bobby Moore held the Jules Rimet Trophy aloft after England's momentous victory over West Germany in the 1966 World Cup Final at Wembley, I was only 5 years old and too young to appreciate the greatest ever triumph of any of the Home Nations. The first World Cup I can remember clearly was the 1970 tournament in Mexico....

MY WORLD CUP DIARIES 1970 -2018
(A selection of memorable moments watched in pubs or from the sofa)

Mexico 70
(Aged 9 ½. Heat and altitude. Grainy TV coverage via satellite)

First ever memory was Brazil's Pele shooting from his own half over Czechoslovakia's keeper Ivo Viktor who was off his line. Ball went just past the post.

England v Brazil group match. Gordon Banks' epic save from Pele header. Bobby Moore and Pele exchanging shirts at the end (after Moore's impeccable defensive display, and Pele being quite simply the greatest player in this fantastic Brazilian team).

Quarter Final. England throw away a 2-0 lead to lose 3-2 to West Germany after extra time. First time I was dejected watching England. Bobby Charlton was substituted at 2-1, soaked in sweat, his comb over hair strands stuck to his forehead in an untidy fashion, in what turned out to be his last international appearance.

Brilliant Brazil beat Italy 4-1 in the Final. Like the rest of the world, I marvelled at their fourth goal. Slick passing and moving from defence to attack by the team - precision pass from Pele to Carlos Alberto – rocket of a shot into the net. Samba time!

West Germany 1974 and Argentina 1978

(England don't qualify for either tournament, Scotland do)

In 74, Scotland were eliminated at the group stage on goal difference even though they didn't lose any of their 3 matches – only beating the defensively inept Zaire 2-0 (compared to Yugoslavia beating them 9-0) ultimately being their undoing.

Once Scotland went home, Holland and Johann Cruyff in particular were my favourites. They made famous the term Total Football (when a player moves out of position, another in his team replaces him to maintain the overall formation) and were a joy to watch. They have since often been called The Best Team to Never Win the World Cup when after a flawless run to the Final they lost to the host nation.

In 78, managed by Ally MacLeod, Scotland had a decent squad. Hopes were high but things went from pre-tournament 'Ole Ola' (the official song of the World Cup squad featuring Rod Stewart, in which they sang about absolutely definitely bringing home the trophy) to fans chanting 'We want wa money back' at MacLeod after just two group games (a defeat to Peru and a draw with Iran - one of the weakest nations). It all clicked in the final group match v Holland that included one of the greatest ever Scotland goals – Archie Gemmill's mazy dribble, nutmeg and lob over the keeper. Not enough though, Scotland out again at the group stage.

Spain 1982

Lacklustre tournament from England.

Scotland eliminated at group stage yet again (the year of Narey's toe poke mentioned in Chapter 5).

Match I enjoyed most was Northern Ireland's gutsy performance and 1-0 win v Spain thanks to Gerry Armstrong's 47 minute goal.

Mexico 1986

Northern Ireland and Scotland go home early – knocked out at group stage. England are on the verge of joining them on an early flight home – need to beat Poland in final group match. In a Gateshead pub, some friends and I watched one of the great England performances –a 3-0 win, a Gary Lineker hat trick with assists from Newcastle's Peter Beardsley.

England eventually go out in the Quarter Final, beaten by Argentina 2-1. Maradona's disgraceful Hand of God first goal and four minutes later his second (a masterful dribble past 5 England players, often called The Goal of the Century).

Denmark's young striker Michael Laudrup was my favourite player at this tournament (although he failed to make it into FIFA's official Team of the Tournament but what do they know).

Italia 90

(The Three Tenors' Nessun Dorma one)

Another group stage exit for Scotland (lowest point was losing 1-0 to Costa Rica)

England and Republic of Ireland in same group – both qualify for Last 16 (Republic thanks to Niall Quinn's dramatic 78th minute equaliser v Holland in final group match)

Last 16 – I cheered as Republic beat Romania in dramatic penalty shoot-out (They lost to Italy in Quarter Final). Everyone in pub in Whickham goes crazy when David Platt scores for England in the last minute of extra time v Belgium.

Semi Final – Heartache in pub in Low Fell, Gateshead as England lose dramatic penalty shoot-out to West Germany. (Chris Waddle sends his pen into orbit. Gazza cries).

USA 1994

(The one where singer Diana Ross missed an open goal in the opening ceremony)

Republic of Ireland are the sole home nation representatives (I fully accept that they are not actually a home nation in football terms but I like to use a bit of artistic licence with them). Watching their group match v Italy in a packed Newcastle pub it seemed that everyone in there was Irish. We celebrated their shock 1-0 win with pints of that traditional dark stout.

France 1998

Opening match of the tournament was Scotland v Brazil. Watched this on a giant screen in a large beer tent on Glasgow Green on a glorious sunny afternoon with two work colleagues. 1-1 at half time, expectations were high and Glaswegians were drunk. Queuing for the toilet at half time, with a chorus 'We Hate the English' ringing out from dozens of them, I managed to safely do what I had to do in there without opening my mouth and giving the game away. National fervour was rising and it was a genuinely scary experience. Scotland went on to lose 2-1 and, of course, went out at the group stage again.

Watched England v Argentina's Last 16 match in Glasgow pub with some Scottish friends. Some people wearing Argentina shirts and some wearing A.B.E. t-shirts (that's to show they are supporting Anyone But England). When Alan Shearer clinically put away his spot-kick and Michael Owen scored his fantastic goal, I had my arms in the air cheering (to find I was one of only half a dozen doing this in the packed pub). The majority of the pub did start to cheer of course when David Batty missed his crucial penalty in the shoot-out and England exited. This was the cue to start the community singing of their adaptation of Skinner and Baddiel's England World Cup song – changed to 'England's Coming Home'. The Scots really have never forgiven the English for having the audacity to win the World Cup in 1966.

South Korea / Japan 2002

On holiday in Mallorca, very early morning drinking with two friends, watched England's final group match v Nigeria in bar in Puerto Pollenca. This match was being shown live on one TV, and Sweden v Argentina (the other final group match taking place at the same time) was being shown on another TV at the other side of the bar. There were fans from all four nations there and it was all harmonious and good natured (England and Sweden qualified for the Last 16).

Germany 2006

With five mates, watched England's opener v Paraguay, drinking shandies, in stifling heat, sitting outside of a pub in Langdale, Lake District. After the match we walked up a mountain.

South Africa 2010

Sole home nation representatives England stumble through their group. In Last 16, I cringe on the sofa as they lose 4-1 to Germany.

Brazil 2014

England are the only home nation in the Finals again, but they catch an early flight home without winning any of their 3 group matches. Best match I watched was Germany beating Brazil 7-1 in Semi Final – 5 goals in the incredible first half hour.

Russia 2018

Anita and I watched Spain v Portugal in a bar in Amsterdam that was packed with Spaniards. Great atmosphere on a beautiful sunny evening. Their evening was spoilt by a late precision free kick from Portugal's Ronaldo to make it 3-3.

Whilst waiting at Amsterdam airport for flight home we watched a match in an airport bar with Muzzy Izzet (the former Leicester City player and Turkish international).

I made a schoolboy error of buying tickets for a show before the World Cup draw was made. When the draw was made, the show turned out to be on the same evening as the England v Belgium group match, so instead of watching the match, I was actually at Kevin and Karen from Strictly Come Dancing's show at the Sage Gateshead with Anita. At one point I was invited onto the stage to dance together with a few other members of the audience. I was already missing the match so I thought I might as well throw myself completely into the dance show. There is a song from 1979 by Sister Sledge called He's The Greatest Dancer. I am the antithesis of this.

A good tournament for England eventually ends in heartache with a Semi Final defeat to Croatia (see fictional account at the start of this chapter).

CHAPTER

HOW IT WAS AND AS IT IS

In just over 50 years of following football, much has changed. Fans who have been on a similar lengthy journey to me will have their own opinions as to whether football was better how it was then or as it is now. Personally I sit firmly on the fence – I like both the olden days and the modern era. Some changes in football during this time have undoubtedly mirrored some of the changing traits in society generally e.g. better living standards, and different personal ambitions and priorities. Football has certainly been a constant feature of my life but it also has been, and still is, a constantly changing one. Here are a few aspects that have changed - and how I have changed with them.

GROUNDS FOR IMPROVEMENT

As a teenager in the 1970s, football grounds did not seem to me to be safe places to visit. Admittedly I only had actual experience of going to St James' Park to watch matches with large crowds, but it was fairly typical of grounds at that time, most of which had not been structurally altered or improved for many decades. It was pretty scary standing on the packed (it could be argued overcrowded) Gallowgate End terrace surrounded by adults who did not seem to care if they crushed you. The police did not seem to care too much about this either. Also, I would only venture into the foul-smelling Gallowgate End outside toilets if absolutely necessary to avoid walking through at times an ankle-deep pool of urine formed by the poor drainage. (When I went to Crystal Palace's Selhurst Park ground in 1983 I was surprised to find outside toilets that smelt worse than the Gallowgate End ones. I would not have believed this without seeing them with my own eyes – and smelling them with my own nose).

The rise of football hooliganism in the 1970s was another concern for me. I have never looked for trouble at, before or after a match, but I have occasionally been unfortunate enough to be on the periphery of outbreaks of fighting between rival groups of fans. That was scary enough for me - I am a flighter not a fighter – a football fan not a football hooligan. In the early 1980s I did once have a handbags type situation in the Gallowgate End with a fellow Toon supporter who was making racist comments and spitting on policemen as they walked up the gangway in the middle of terrace. That is the sum total of my football violence – and it wasn't even with a rival fan. Hooliganism developed at some clubs into organised gangs (firms, casuals, crew etc) but it was, and thankfully still is, only a small part of the beautiful game's culture.

A tragic consequence of the upkeep neglect and lack of health and safety at football stadiums back then happened at Bradford City's Valley Parade ground on Saturday 11th May 1985. Fifty six spectators lost their lives in a fire that engulfed a wooden roofed stand, started by a discarded but still lit cigarette that fell through a gap in the floor of the stand onto a large pile of litter under it. Following the Hillsborough disaster on 15th April 1989, when ninety six Liverpool fans were killed in a fatal crush on the Leppings Lane standing-only terrace, the Taylor Report led to the compulsory requirement of all-seater stadiums in the top leagues in England and Scotland by 1994. The tragedies of Bradford and Hillsborough highlighted the danger and, let's be honest, the squalor of most football grounds, and resulted in improved safety, comfort and facilities.

When I returned to the North East in 2000 after my time in Glasgow, St James' Park had changed beyond recognition. The former Leazes End standing terrace behind one of the goals (opposite the Gallowgate End) was now the three tier all seated Sir John Hall Stand. I sat in the back row of this stand for my first visit following my return (Newcastle versus Charlton Athletic on Saturday 23rd September 2000). After climbing 15 flights of stairs, the players looked so small from this elevated vantage point that it seemed like I was looking down onto a Subbuteo match. Soon after this, I secured my season ticket for the seat with a great view of the pitch in the Milburn Stand (as detailed in Chapter 3). Compared to how it used to be, St James' Park was now an impressive modern stadium that felt less forbidding and certainly more welcoming towards women and children. I am happy that the era of foul smelling outside toilets and being pushed around on the crumbling terraces has gone – but, like a lot of football fans my age, every so often I have a strange feeling of loss and hanker after a return to the old days.

FROM RARE OCCASION TO SKY INVASION

As detailed in Chapter 2, the 1968 FA Cup Final was the first live match I watched on TV. There were very few televised live football matches in the 1960s but the English FA Cup Final was a guaranteed live annual broadcast. It was invariably the last match of the domestic football season and was a major television event at that time, with an audience of millions from all over the world. Not only was the whole match broadcast live (except for viewers in Scotland who received the whole of the Scottish Cup Final that took place at the same time) but there were also other Cup Final related features for hours before and after it. For example, before the kick off the TV cameras would follow each team leaving their hotel (that was usually just outside of London) and a reporter would travel with and interview them as their team bus headed to Wembley. At the stadium, you could watch the players in their suits wandering around the pitch – getting a feel for the Wembley turf. There would be interviews with celebrity and non-celebrity fans of both teams and various fun events filmed previously (e.g. It's A Cup Final Knockout, A Cup Final Question of Sport). Prior to kick off you could watch the traditional singing of Abide With Me, maybe introduced by Bruce Forsyth or a similar type of celebrity, and the teams lining up to be introduced to a member of the Royal Family. After the match, you could watch the presentation of the cup and medals, the winning team running around the Wembley pitch wearing hats and scarves their fans had draped over them as they were going up the stairs to receive the Cup, and the joker member of the team would probably have the lid of the cup balanced on his head whilst doing some crazy dance. The cameras would then be allowed into the dressing rooms where you could watch the players in the communal bath, some drinking champagne out of the FA Cup and some drinking milk out of glass bottles. Both before and after the match, all this action would be interspersed with analysis and comments from the football pundits back in the studio.

There were also football highlights shows on television in the 1960s. On a Saturday night the BBC broadcasted highlights of some of that afternoon's First Division games in Match of the Day and on Sunday ITV's The Big Match showed extended highlights of a game from the previous day. However, with the odd exception of some live international matches or European ties involving a British club, that was how it was for televised football matches back then.

How different it is now. In the current world of satellite broadcasting and subscription channels, you are able to watch live football matches from all over the world at various times of the day every day of the week. It all started in 1991 with the subscription satellite TV channel Sky Sports. Not insubstantial Sky money paid to mainly top flight clubs to broadcast their live matches, assisted them in their ground improvements, or helped them to finance the building of new stadiums. The money talked very persuasively. For the 1992/93 season, Sky influenced the clubs in the top division to move away from the English Football League set up to form the Premier League. There was also a move away from all Premier League matches kicking off at 3pm on Saturday to selected matches each weekend being played on Sunday afternoons and Monday evenings for live transmission on Sky Sports. Other similar channels followed – ESPN, Setanta, Premier Sports, BT Sport to name but a few.

Pre-Sky Sports, it would be highly unlikely for a professional football match to take place on a Sunday. In the 2010s, it is in theory possible to watch live football on TV all day on any given Sunday. You could start at 1am with a couple of live Major League Soccer matches from the USA to see you through until breakfast time. A live fixture from the Australian A League at around 8am could be up next (Newcastle Jets are in this league, they would clearly have to be My One Side of Australia). Late morning you may have a match from Seria A in Italy (maybe involving one of the Milan teams or Juventus) or you could choose a (with the greatest of respect) slightly less glamourous game taking place in Scotland at the same time (Ross County v St Mirren anyone?). By 2 pm Sky will be transmitting their showcase two Super Sunday live games. Do not be too disappointed to have to watch Huddersfield v Watford first because the match they have been plugging all week, with movie style trailers, as The Clash of the Titans or The Match of the Century or something similar, will be live at 4pm. If by 4.30 pm Arsenal v Chelsea has not lived up to its top billing, do not despair because around this time on a Sunday you will certainly be able to find other live matches to watch on other satellite channels (maybe from the German Bundesliga or Dutch Eredivisie leagues). Your Sunday evening football fix will usually be live matches from the French Ligue or Spanish La Liga. Approaching midnight, you may be a bit tired of watching football but if not you might be able to squeeze one more match in before you nod off if there is some live South American football from say Brazil or Argentina on an obscure subscription channel.

Living in the United Kingdom and being able to watch extensive live football from all over Europe and beyond is a welcome development from the how it was scarcity of live football on TV. I am sure most would agree that sitting on your sofa with a can of beer and a bowl of crisps is not as good as actually being at a match, but the growth in live TV coverage allows football fans who for whatever reason are unable to regularly attend matches to enjoy the excitement of the beautiful game in comfort and at their convenience. This can only be a good thing.

THE RISE OF THE WOMEN'S GAME

Girls don't play football. That is how it was during my schooldays and early adulthood. At school, boys played football and girls played netball. The sexes would only join together to play rounders. Much as I enjoyed watching the 1981 coming of age comedy film Gregory's Girl, where teenager Dorothy initially encounters scepticism and sexism before being accepted onto the boys' school football team and outplaying them, I still thought it's only a film and football is still a male only sport. It was the 1990s before I personally encountered women playing football seriously. This was in Glasgow when I was one of 8 males and 2 females who played 5 a side together every week. The ladies were certainly as physically fit as the men but less skilled. I found myself letting them have more time on the ball and not tackling them too hard. I also had to try hard not to laugh on the number of occasions that one of them kicked thin air rather than the ball. In 2005 I regularly played 5 a side in Newcastle with work colleagues. Sometimes a female colleague played, and she was just as fast, tough and skilful as the males, and she wanted to be treated no differently. I was in my mid-forties and I had only now encountered my first proper female footballer.

When reading about women's football, I was surprised to learn that in 1881 a Scotland-England international match between two teams of women took place at Easter Road, Edinburgh. I also discovered that women's football leagues were played in England during the First World War but were then banned by the FA in 1921 for 50 years who deemed that football was unsuitable for females (in 2008 the FA apologised for the ban – after 87 years, better late than never I suppose). The English Women's FA was formed in 1969 (England's men winning the 1966 World Cup generally increased interest in the game). The first FIFA Women's World Cup was held in China in 1991. During the 21st Century, women's football has grown in popularity with wider participation in all age groups.

I feel ashamed to say it is only during the 2010s that I have taken an interest in the women's game, but I console myself that there are a large number of male football fans (some of whom I know personally) who still do not accept that women's football is a proper sport. Their main bugbear seems to be that the women's game is too slow and therefore boring to watch. To me this is a poor excuse for not watching it. There are some clear physical differences between men and women. Men are, in general, stronger and quicker. In tennis, this is the reason why men play 5 sets and women only play 3. In athletics sprint and long-distance races, the men's world records are all considerably faster than the women's. If my fellow male football supporters can become more enlightened and accept these basic truths, they may find they will start to enjoy watching women's football after all.

Saturday 11th May 2019
Durham Women v Tottenham Hotspur Ladies
New Ferens Park, Belmont, Durham

The first women's match I attended was in 2019. I went with friends Vince and Caroline Ryan whose 17-year-old daughter Chloe was on the bench for Durham Women. It was the last match of the season in the FA Women's Championship.

Spurs Ladies had just secured promotion to the FA Women's Super League and Durham Women had narrowly missed out. Two second half headed goals by Anna Filbey gave Spurs a 2-0 win in a very competitive match. There were no signs of they're already on the beach going on here. I bought a programme and was given a free Panini Women's World Cup 2019 sticker album and packet of stickers (another good example of how popular women's football had become). The attendance was 533.

Today's England internationals like Jill Scott and Lucy Bronze are great role models both on and off the pitch for any young girl aspiring to be a footballer. Current England captain Steph Houghton is every bit as passionate at leading her country as her iconic male counterparts Bobby Moore and Bryan 'Captain Marvel' Robson were. She too is a great ambassador for the evolving women's game. I have friends whose daughters are showing great promise – Chloe Ryan has played for England Schoolgirls – and they are actively encouraging them in their ambition to make the grade. I am pleased that is now as it is. It would never have happened how it was back in my day.

FLICKING LITTLE PLASTIC MEN

As a teenager in the 1970s, kicking a ball around a grass pitch was not the only football I played back then. When the weather was too bad to play outdoors, like most young lads who were mad about football in those days, I played the indoor Subbuteo variety instead. This involved flicking little plastic men around a green baize pitch for hours on end with my younger brother and other friends. One particular game I can remember that completely illustrated both the pleasures and perils of playing this miniature version of football was when one of my friends and I were playing an Anglo-Scottish Cup competition. The two-legged Final was Newcastle versus Aberdeen. Both Toon fans, we had a friendly argument (that I lost) over who would be Newcastle. The first leg was played at his house, on his parents' dining room table. There were no major incidents and Newcastle won 3-1. The second leg took place the next day at my house. With no suitable table to put the pitch on, we had to play on the floor of my small bedroom. Approaching half time, Aberdeen were back in the tie with a 2-0 lead. My mam then opened the bedroom door, stood on one of my players and told us we would have to stop the match because she needed to hoover the floor, and no it couldn't wait until we had finished the Subbuteo match because she needed to do it now, and she had a 101 other things to do, and no it didn't matter that this was the crucial second leg of the Anglo-Scottish Cup Final. She bundled up the pitch scattering all the players. Half an hour later we were allowed to set up the pitch on my bedroom floor again. A Manchester United Subbuteo player came on a substitute for the broken Aberdeen player who would need to be glued back onto his base by my dad later – hopefully not a career ending injury for him. We started playing again but my rhythm had been upset, and my friend's Newcastle team made a comeback. It finished 3-2 to Aberdeen, meaning Newcastle won 5-4 on aggregate. I suppose one consolation was Newcastle actually winning a trophy for a change. During 1973/74 my obsession with Subbuteo saw me play, either with friends or solo, the entire World Cup qualifying matches (from Europe, South America, North/Central America, Asia and Africa). Unlike in the real world of football, Guatemala and Cyprus qualified for the 1974 World Cup Finals in Germany. Order was restored in the Finals with Brazil the eventual winners.

Breaking players by kneeling or standing on them then gluing them back together, matches being abandoned after interruptions by your parents, and crazy results that are highly unlikely to happen in real life football (Scotland winning the World Cup for example, or even just getting out of their group to reach the knock out stages) - some of the beauty of Subbuteo.

People born after the 1970s might struggle to understand the wide appeal of Subbuteo back in the day (although interestingly the game has had a surge in popularity again in recent years). It was a kind of forerunner to today's popular FIFA Football video games, where flicking little plastic men around a pitch has been replaced by remotely controlling the movements of computer-generated images of today's top footballers. I found it a lot easier to master the flick to kick technique of Subbuteo than my many failed attempts to master the controls of a gaming console needed to play FIFA Football (this is probably just an age thing to be honest).

Football video games I have had more success with are the Championship Manager type ones, where your tactical abilities and skills in the transfer market are tested as boss of a team. In this game, if you are skilful enough, you can take Rochdale from the fourth tier of English football to winning the UEFA Champions League in 5 seasons – although your team will now have Neymar, Sergio Ramos, Raheem Stirling etc in it rather than actual Rochdale players of course.

Whether playing Subbuteo how it was or video games as it is, there is no denying that when you cannot for whatever reason play or watch football outdoors, there are some great indoor alternatives to ease the pain.

THE GOAL MINER AND THE MILLIONAIRES

Jackie Milburn was a Newcastle United legend from 1943 to 1957. Only Alan Shearer scored more goals in his Newcastle playing career (from 1996 to 2006) than him. Milburn worked as a coal miner prior to joining Newcastle United and continued to do so after joining the club. There were times when he would work a double shift at Woodhorn Colliery, Ashington on a Friday to enable him to play for Newcastle at 3pm the next day. This seems incredible when nowadays we hear that so and so is tired after a match went to extra time and he had to play for 120 minutes not 90, or that so and so is tired because he has played three matches in eight days. It could be argued, and correctly I would say, that the pace of today's game is quicker than in Milburn's day, but would Lionel Messi be able to do his quick mazy dribbling runs after swinging a pick axe at a coalface only hours before? Jackie Milburn is a great example of how it was for even the best players in his day.

When my interest in football started in the late 1960s /early 1970s, most professional footballers were not household names. There were a few exceptions – Bobbys Moore and Charlton for example were not only great players but generally considered to be suitable role models for aspiring youngsters. George Best was probably the first celebrity footballer, although he was as equally famous for his love of drinking, nightclubbing and dating models or actresses, as for his incredible football talent.

Over the years the substantial money being ploughed into the game, from sponsorship deals, TV broadcasting rights etc, means today's typical Premier League footballer earns eye watering amounts of dosh for kicking a ball around – with an average weekly salary that is double the average UK worker's annual salary. Due to the increased interest in the game and the proliferation of social media, a greater number of footballers than ever before have become celebrities of sorts, particularly the ones whose wives or girlfriends are also celebrities of sorts (e.g. members of girl bands, actresses in TV soaps or glamour models).

As it is now, even if there was still a coalmining industry in the UK, footballers would not need to work underground as Jackie Milburn did to supplement their income from football to make ends meet. Most Premier League players' salaries are over £1 million per annum, with the top players earning multiple millions each season. Players at Championship and Leagues 1 and 2 clubs are paid less of course but they still generally earn six figure sums. Being a professional footballer is certainly lucrative, but it is also brief, with a playing career usually all over by 40 at the latest. I am comfortable that they are paid similarly to other top entertainers (actors and directors in the movie business for example) and other top sports stars. However, as detailed in Chapter 3, in the 2010s I gradually became less interested in going to watch Newcastle United in the Premier League and found watching non-league football at Gateshead a better all-round experience for me. I still watch Premier League and Championship matches on TV and very much enjoy doing so, but in 2018 I decided to embark on a new live football watching venture – the non-league non-professional level game.

"THE REFEREE CHECKS HIS WATCH….

…and signals the end of the first half".

(Back to the studio for first half analysis from an ex-player called Gary, Macca, Stevie or something similar) *"It started with young Michael catching the football bug and supporting his two sides of the Tyne – Newcastle United and Gateshead. He has watched them a lot – not sure how many times exactly but it is in triple figures for both teams. Midway through the first half there was a good spell in Scotland. He also reminisced about playing football in his younger years, watching the World Cup and his Tyne and Weirdo Sunderland thing. Towards the end of the half, he reflected on how the game had changed from when he started watching it fifty years earlier.*

After the half time interval, he will be emerging for the second half, older but still enthusiastic, with a different football watching routine…"

HALF TIME

It is time to take a fifteen minute break. If that last pint of lager you quickly finished off just before the kick-off caused you a bit of discomfort towards the end of the first half, a dash to the toilet will be in order. It is also an opportunity to buy some food and drink without missing any of the action. Alternatively, you may just want to read the matchday programme….

GATECASTLE UNITED FC

Official Matchday Programme (Number 666)

Versus SOMETOWN UNITED
Northerly League Premier Division
Saturday 12th of Never 2020

CHAIRMAN'S CHATTER
from Barry Ireland

There's More Than One United !

We bid a warm welcome to players, officials and supporters from our local rivals Sometown United today. This clash of two United's is a reminder that there is more than one team called United in the wonderful game of football. Those of you who know me well know that it is a major bugbear of mine when people refer to Manchester United as just United. The main culprits are television and radio pundits, former Manchester United players and their fans. The likes of Gary Neville, Paul Scholes and Michael Owen are good examples. (N.B. I have purposely written 'the likes of' here as this is actually another bugbear of mine. A number of pundits, including these three, but they are by no means the only ones, often talk about the likes of Gareth Bale or the Mo Salahs of this world rather than just saying Gareth Bale or Mo Salah. It gets on my nerves but I am digressing, let's get back to my major bugbear....).

I know Manchester United are a great club with a proud history but I think constantly calling them just United is an insult to Newcastle, West Ham, Leeds, Sheffield, Scunthorpe, Peterborough, Oxford, Carlisle, Marske, Hyde and all the many other Uniteds. OK rant over for this week! I hope I haven't upset too many people in Manchester (come to think of it though, given Manchester United's fan base profile, I have likely upset more people in Surrey and Asia with these comments than in Manchester).

Back to today's Gatecastle-Sometown Derby match in the Northerly League. As well as giving us the very important local bragging rights, a win could also lift us into the promotion places. So, may the best team win....we all know that is Gatecastle United of course!

Enjoy the game!

BARRY

MANAGER'S MUTTERINGS
from Robbie Dobson

Get behind the lads!

We go into today's game on the back of three straight wins. I was particularly pleased with the way we ground out a 4-3 win at West Eastford last week in what was a pulsating end-to-end thriller of a match. Unfortunately, we picked up a few injuries during it. Biggsy (groin) and Thommo (knee) are both out for today, and Bruiser also picked up an injury off the field (glass cut on his neck) at Kasablanca's night club in the town on Saturday night celebrating the win (He should be fine after being stitched up, not for the first time in his life, at the Gatecastle Infirmary in the early hours of Sunday morning). I am leaving him out of the team today though because he does tend to get sent off early on in derby matches with Sometown anyway.

This will give youngsters Pixie, Shorty and 'Breast Milk' the chance to start a match and prove themselves. I know you will get right behind them and give them and all the lads your full vocal support.

Come on Gatecastle!!

ROBBIE

Where the love match with football began. An 8 pitch outdoor 5-a-side complex is now on the site of Gateshead FC's long gone Redheugh Park ground.

Champions of Gateshead 1972. The author aged 11 is on the extreme right of the middle row.

The Vase and Two Bananas. Better known as the Inter Cities Fairs Cup.
The last significant trophy won by Newcastle United - 51 years ago

A regular view over the decades for the author from the
Tyne and Wear Stand at Gateshead International Stadium

*Gateshead FC have their name in lights at Wembley Stadium
for the first time on 18th May 2014*

*Some shirts of the two sides of the Tyne. Just to be different, the author generally favoured
buying away shirts rather than the more popular home ones*

When you are the first winners of the World Cup (57 years before England) you can be forgiven for bragging about it!

Newcastle Benfield fans entering the turnstile at Guisborough Town (29th December 2018)

West Auckland's Amar Purewal neatly despatches a penalty in their match at Hebburn Town on 16th February 2019

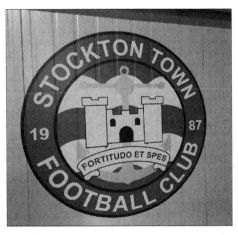

Northern League Division 1 Mission accomplished on 20th March 2019 at Stockton Town

Trainspotting inspired poster at the entrance to Heaton Stannington FC perfectly summing up all that is good about watching non-league football

Picturesque backdrop at Redcar Athletic v Crook Town (7th September 2019)

Anything Beckham can do.....Chester-le-Street Town v Carlisle City (4th January 2020)

Journey's End at Jarrow. Overall Mission to visit all the grounds in the Northern League Divisions 1 and 2 completed on 12th September 2020 at Jarrow's Perth Green ground for their match against Durham City.

*Some groundhopping essentials plus a selection of programmes
from the matches featured in The Second Half*

MY GAME OF TWO HALVES

THE SECOND HALF
The Diary of a Groundhopper
(aged 50 something)

CHAPTER

THE NOVICE HOPPER

The woodpecker.

The treecreeper.

The rockhopper penguin.

The groundhopper?

It seems to me that the groundhopper could easily belong to the bird family. If a groundhopper was a bird I reckon its characteristics would be;

Scientific name - Footballae ubiquitous

Habitat - Any football ground anywhere, ranging from luxurious large all-seater stadiums to roped-off no-seater unlevel muddy pitches.

Identification - Easy to spot as usually carrying a notebook and/or a camera. May also be wearing a coat or beanie hat with pin badges on, collected from visits to a variety of clubs

Wingspan - At most non-league grounds with lower crowds, have the space to move around and watch from both left and right wings (and behind both goals) during the 90 minutes

Food - Mainly of the 'fast' variety, including pies, chips, burgers and hot dogs. Infrequently salad.

In 2018, I decided to join the family of groundhoppers.

AROUND THE NORTHERN LEAGUE GROUNDS
(Part 1 - August to November 2018)

August 2018.

After working for over 40 years I have just retired. Early.

Retirement meant that I would, in theory, have more time to watch football. The 2018/19 season was just commencing so I decided to choose a league and attempt to visit the grounds of all the teams in that league during the season. In short, I wanted to be a groundhopper. A very late in the day groundhopper but a groundhopper all the same.

I chose the Northern League Division 1, the majority of whose 18 clubs were based in North East England. This is Level 9 of the English Football League Pyramid (where Level 1 is the Premier League i.e. the highest professional league, and Level 5 is the National League i.e. the highest level of non-league). This would be a good challenge, particularly travelling to the outlier clubs like Penrith and Guisborough from my Newcastle upon Tyne home base. It would mean an average of 2 new grounds per month to visit during the season, and I should still be able to attend some Gateshead home games. I had only previously visited one of these 18 grounds (Whitley Bay in 2009 for their pre-season friendly with Gateshead).

Established in 1889, the Northern League is the world's second oldest football league still in existence, after the English Football League which was formed a year earlier. Bishop Auckland, one of the clubs competing in the 2018/19 league season, played in the Northern League's inaugural 1889/90 season. Eight other clubs in the 2018/19 Division 1 have histories stretching back over 100 years, founded in proud mining, shipbuilding, railway working and steel working towns and villages. These once thriving North East industries have sadly declined in these places, but I was to discover that the football clubs are still at the heart of the communities. Football at this level is a far cry from the relative glamour of the Premier League but it has its own culture with loyally supported clubs, albeit by hundreds of fans rather than thousands or tens of thousands.

After half a century of mainly watching football in the twin arenas of St James' Park and Gateshead International Stadium, I spread my groundhopper wings on journeys via buses, trains and automobiles, travelling around Tyneside, Wearside and County Durham to watch what turned out to be some lower level but highly enjoyable football, ticking off the 18 grounds.

I called this The Mission.

......MISSION.......POSSIBLE.........

DERBY DAY AT RCA
Northern League Ground 1

Saturday 4th August 2018
SUNDERLAND RCA
Meadow Park, Ryhope, Sunderland, Tyne and Wear

Formed in 1963 as Ryhope Youth Club and played in the Seaham and District League. In 1971 changed name to Ryhope Community Association. Folded 1975, reformed 1978 and played in the Northern Alliance. In 1982 the club was a founder member of Northern League Division 2. In 1999 amalgamated with Kennet Roker and in 2006/07 season became Sunderland Ryhope Community Association FC – now commonly known as Sunderland RCA.

Best league performance – 4th place in Northern League Division 1 (2011/12 and 2017/18)

Northern League Division 2 runners-up (1983/84 and 2009/10)

I have always enjoyed the opening day of a new football season. Admittedly the very entertaining World Cup Finals in Russia on TV during June and July helped to make the 2018 close season pass quicker, but the arrival of Saturday 4th August and the start of the 2018/19 season was most welcome.

There is always the feeling on the opening day that it is a new start for the team you support and anything is possible, including winning whatever league they play in. After all, the slate is clean; it's all to play for. That is the theory. In practice as I have detailed in The First Half of this book, when supporting Newcastle and Gateshead that bubble soon bursts.

Sunderland's relegation to English Football League 1 at the end of the 2017/18 season put two divisions between them and local Premier League rivals Newcastle. The prospect of a Tyne-Wear derby match in the near future looked remote but the opening day Northern League Division 1 fixtures included a non-league version of the Tyne-Wear derby. Sunderland RCA and Newcastle Benfield were two of the top teams in Division 1 last season, finishing 4th and 7th respectively.

My travelling companion to Meadow Park was Kev Larkham. We had worked at the same bank for many years, and with my upcoming early retirement at the end of this month, we had vowed to stay in touch and do some groundhopping together. Kev is a few years younger than me so sadly for him retirement is a bit further away. He has watched many Northern League games in recent years and has a good knowledge of the league. We travelled via public transport and public houses from Newcastle to Ryhope with the buzz of the start of the season in the air. We encountered Newcastle United fans on our way heading to St James' Park for the pre-season friendly with German side Augsburg. Their black and white striped tops looked pristine – newly washed and ironed – and, like us, I am sure they were looking forward to a good day out watching football in the sunshine. (It turned out to be not such a good day on the pitch for The Toon - they played poorly and lost 1-0).

On arriving at RCA's Meadow Park ground, we learnt that Sunderland had beaten Charlton Athletic 2-1 in their League 1 lunchtime kick-off opening match. The winning goal was scored in the 96th minute and some RCA players, clearly Sunderland supporters, interrupted their pre-match warm up to celebrate.

Just before kick-off, a stray ball from the warm up landed a few yards in front of me at the side of the pitch. I dribbled the ball a bit and then hit it with my left foot back onto the pitch, narrowly missing a couple standing on the touchline. I apologised and the man said it was no problem but I think it may have been if the ball had hit his wife on the head (it missed by inches). Maybe I should have used my favoured right foot.

The match was a good contest between two evenly matched teams. The home side probably just edged the first half but it was goalless at the interval. It was settled by a well taken 48th minute goal from veteran Benfield striker Paul Brayson (who had played for a number of clubs in his 20 year football career including my own two sides of the Tyne).

We encountered two typical non-league fans (I would point out that I call them that with absolute affection) amongst the crowd. There was a RCA fan who told us that even though it was a blazing hot sunny day with no rain forecast he had brought his waterproof jacket just in case. Another fan wearing an Oxford University sweatshirt had not actually attended that esteemed seat of learning (as we had guessed) - he just liked the design.

Vital Statistics:

Sunderland RCA 0 Newcastle Benfield 1 (Brayson 48)

Northern League Division 1

Admission - £6

Programme - £1

Attendance – 110

……..MISSION……COMMENCED……..

Although my main focus was on The Mission, I still wanted to attend as many Gateshead matches as possible during the season.

After a summer of uncertainty, with boardroom upheaval and a switch to part time basis resulting in an exodus of most of last season's squad, thankfully National League football resumed at the GIS with the visit of newly promoted big spending Salford City. I had not been to any of Gateshead's pre-season friendlies, so I was looking forward to seeing Steve Watson's new young team in action for the first time.

Anita and I arrived at the ground about 20 minutes before kick-off and found it to be remarkably busy. I probably need to explain this further. In all my years of attending Gateshead home games, small crowds have been a regular feature, with only the odd notable exception (The National League Play Off Semi Final Second Leg versus Grimsby Town in May 2014 for example, as detailed in Chapter 3). The average home attendance during the 2017/18 season was 853. So, it did seem a bit unusual that we were told by a steward that the part of the Tyne and Wear Stand we normally sit in was getting a bit full and could we move down to another entrance. Anita bought two 50-50 half time draw tickets that turned out to be a good investment, as one of them was the winning ticket and we went home after the match £155 richer.

We took our seats at the other end of the stand. Ex-Manchester United players Paul Scholes, Ryan Giggs, Nicky Butt and the Neville brothers each have a 10% shareholding in Salford City, and Anita was hoping that one of them would be in the director's box tonight. They weren't. Actor Jimmy Nail was though (but that was no consolation apparently).

The match started badly for The Heed when on 11 minutes Adam Rooney, Salford's close season signing from Aberdeen headed home. The Heed looked to be giving Salford too much respect in the opening period and almost conceded a second goal - Rooney hitting the bar on the half hour. Heed Manager Steve Watson was getting increasingly frustrated – at one point punching the dugout (bet that hurt). Gateshead then started getting some joy on the wings, forcing a few corners. On 37 minutes, winger Cameron Salkeld was brought down as he blazed into the box. Luke Armstrong coolly despatched the penalty kick. So at half time the underdogs/relegation favourites had deservedly drawn level with the money bags/promotion favourites.

Gateshead started the second half where they left off in the first, increasing in confidence all the time. On 68 minutes Armstrong scored his second goal. A late scare on 85 minutes when Salford hit the post would have been cruel on The Heed, who overall thoroughly deserved the win.

Vital Statistics:

Gateshead 2 (Armstrong 37 pen, 68) Salford City 1 (Rooney 11)

National League

Admission - £15

Programme – sold out

Attendance – 1,243 (98 away fans)

ONE MAN AND HIS DOG
Northern League Ground 2

Saturday 18th August 2018
SHILDON
Dean Street, Shildon, County Durham

Founded in 1890 as Shildon Town and played in the Auckland and District League. In 1894 merged with The Rangers And Heroes to become Shildon United, folded in 1900, reformed in 1903 as Shildon FC and joined the Northern League. Nicknamed The Railwaymen after the wagon works that served the Stockton and Darlington Railway in the golden age of steam locomotion from 1833. The wagon works remained a major employer in the town until its closure in 1984.

Northern League Division 1 winners (1933/34, 1934/35, 1935/36, 1936/37, 1939/40 and 2015/16) Division 2 winners (2001/02)

Northern League Cup winners (1933/34, 1934/35, 1937/38, 1938/39, 1939/40, 1952/53, 2002/03, 2014/15 and 2015/16)

Durham Challenge Cup winners (1907/08, 1925/26, 2013/14 and 2014/15)

Last time in FA Cup 1st Round Proper (2003/04)

FA Vase semi-finalists (2012/13)

Next up was a trip to Shildon, who were well established in the Northern League's top flight. Kev Larkham and I visited a pub near to the ground prior to kick-off. Some guests from a nearby wedding came in to watch Cardiff v Newcastle, the early kick-off match on Sky Sports, on the big screen. Hopefully their special day improved after it because it was a poor goalless draw. When Newcastle's Kenedy missed a 95th minute penalty it was just too much for one young lad who started stamping on his mobile phone (I am guessing he may have had a bet on a 1-0 win for The Toon). We walked up to the ground and entered the turnstile behind three people carrying boxes of fish and chips they had just bought at the nearby chip shop. This would not be allowed at a Premier League ground that is for sure.

We sat in the newly built Creed Capital Stand, which was housing a mix of Shildon and visiting Benfield fans. The visitors took the lead on 18 minutes – a well taken goal from Dale Pearson. Shildon's Matty Robson equalised 3 minutes later, and they took a 2-1 lead into half time from a Ben Trotter goal on the half hour mark. For the second half, we moved out of the stand and onto the touchline near to the goal that Benfield were attacking. They put the home side's defence under some pressure in the first 15 minutes of the second half, but it was a Benfield defensive error on 68 minutes latched onto by Shildon's Jack Blackford that extended their lead to 3-1. Benfield kept attacking though and there was some desperate defending in the home goalmouth at times, and a lot of abuse being directed at the linesman from Shildon's keeper about his decisions. We were standing behind the linesman and Kev asked him whether he was going to stand for all that abuse. He took heed of Kev's advice and the next time a torrent came his way he told the keeper to keep quiet. That was a great example of non-league supporter and official interaction. Pearson scored a late second goal for Benfield but Shildon held on.

It is a cliché that some non-league matches are watched by just one man and his dog. The attendance was 273, but this did not include the actual one man and his dog that we spotted watching from the window of their house overlooking the ground. It looks like he has a free season ticket for as long as he lives there.

Vital Statistics:

Shildon 3 (Robson 21, Trotter 32, Blackford 68)

Newcastle Benfield 2 (Pearson 18, 88)

Northern League Division 1

Admission - £6

Programme – £2

Attendance – 273 or 275 (depending on counting measure used)

GAZZA'S OLD HAUNT
Northern League Ground 3

Wednesday 22nd August 2018
DUNSTON UTS
The UTS Stadium, Wellington Road, Dunston

Formed in 1975 as Whickham Sports FC and played in the Northern Amateur League. Joined the Northern Combination League in 1980. Changed name to Dunston Mechanics FC in 1982. Federation Brewery became the club's main sponsor in 1987 and name was changed to Dunston Federation Brewery FC (they became known as The Fed). Won the Northern Combination League and Cup in 1987 and joined the Wearside League. They joined the Northern League Division 2 in 1991 and were promoted to Division 1 as Champions in 1992/93 season.

Best league performance – Northern League Division 1 champions (2003/04 and 2004/05).

FA Vase Winners (2011/12)

Northern League Cup winners (1997/98, 1998/99, 1999/2000, 2003/04, 2004/05 and 2017/18)

Best FA Cup performance – Final Qualifying Round (2003/04 and 2018/19 when they lost 4-0 to Gateshead)

Anita accompanied me to this Wednesday 7.30 pm kick-off match – Dunston's opponents were Seaham Red Star. It was a lovely summer evening as we took our seats on the not very comfortable wooden planks of the 150 seater UTS Stand (Local business UTS Engineering being the current club sponsors). It was previously called the Paul Gascoigne Stand, in tribute to Dunston's most famous son, until it was destroyed in a fire and rebuilt.

As previously stated, Anita is a Sunderland supporter, our marriage proving that love can sometimes conquer the great divide between Newcastle and Sunderland fans. Throughout tonight's match she spent a fair amount of time checking her mobile phone for score updates on the Gillingham v Sunderland match taking place at Priestfield Stadium. Sunderland won 4-1 so she was happy. This in turn makes my life much easier.

Seaham's Lee Hetherington opened the scoring after 14 minutes, but Dunston levelled five minutes later via an Anthony Myers own goal. On 27 minutes a Dunston penalty kick, taken by Jake Stafford, was well saved by Seaham's larger than life keeper Andy Hunter. It remained level at half time. Dunston started the second half brightly and Mark Fitzpatrick gave them the lead on 51 minutes. Scott Heslop made it 3-1 after 57 minutes, his scorching shot sailing past Hunter into the top of the net, nestling in the left side stanchion. Red Star looked defeated, and Dunston looked the fitter side as they saw the game out for a deserved win.

This was the first ever Northern League match Anita had attended. She said she had really enjoyed it, but I wonder if she would have felt that way if Sunderland had lost tonight.

Vital Statistics:

Dunston UTS 3 (Myers og 19, Fitzpatrick 51, Heslop 57)

Seaham Red Star 1 (Hetherington 14)

Northern League Division 1

Admission - £6

Programme – £1

Attendance – 222

JESUS KEEGAN
Northern League Ground 4

Saturday 1st September 2018
NEWCASTLE BENFIELD
Sam Smith's Park, Benfield Road, Newcastle upon Tyne

Formed in 1988 as Brunswick Village FC and played in Northern Alliance Division 2. Changed name to Heaton Corner House FC the next season, and were champions of Northern Alliance Division 2 in 1989/90. Next season changed name to Newcastle Benfield Park and moved to current stadium. Promoted as runners up in Northern Alliance Division 1 in 1993/94 and won Northern Alliance Premier Division and Cup in 1994/95. Merged with North Shields St Columbas in 1999 and changed name to Newcastle Benfield Saints. Northern Alliance Premier Division champions (2002/03) and promoted to Northern League Division 2. Runners up in Division 2 (2003/04) and promoted to Division 1. In 2005 changed name to Newcastle Benfield Bay Plastics. From 2007 known as Newcastle Benfield. Nicknamed The Lions.

Northern League Division 1 champions and Cup winners 2008/09. Northern League Cup winners (2006/07 and 2010/11)

FA Vase quarter finalists 2013/14.

Best FA Cup performance is Final Qualifying Round.

After recently moving house, Newcastle Benfield are Kev's nearest Northern League team and his 2018/19 season's groundhopping plan was now to follow them at home and away. We had some pre-match refreshment in a nearby pub and in the Benfield clubhouse. There is a great mural in the clubhouse labelled Uncle Alb's Corner depicting a variation of The Last Supper with Kevin Keegan as Jesus and other Newcastle United managers from Joe Harvey (boss when The Toon won the Fairs Cup in 1969) onwards as the apostles.

We watched the first half in the sunshine at the edge of the pitch near to the stand that Benfield bought from Colchester United when they moved from their Layer Road ground in 2008. For the second half we moved to what is known as the Gym Terrace behind the clubhouse goal. Benfield are the only Northern League club to have its own gym in their ground and very impressive it looks too. We had some good craic with the handful of regular home fans on the Gym Terrace and some sporting banter with nearby Stockton fans.

The match itself was pretty forgettable. Two second half headed goals by captain Adam Nicholson secured the 3 points for Stockton who I thought overall deserved their win.

Vital Statistics:

Newcastle Benfield 0 Stockton Town 2 (Nicholson 48, 75)
Northern League Division 1
Admission - £6,
Programme – £1
Attendance – 137

AT THE HOME OF A WORLD CUP WINNER

Northern League Ground 5

Saturday 22nd September 2018
WEST AUCKLAND TOWN
Wanted Stadium, Darlington Road, West Auckland, County Durham

Formed in 1893 as West Auckland FC and played in Wear Valley League, South Durham Alliance and Mid Durham League until 1908 when they joined the Northern League.

Northern League Division 1 Champions (1959/60, 1960/61),

Northern League Cup winners (1958/59, 1962/63),

Durham Challenge Cup Winners (1963/64),

FA Amateur Cup Finalists (1960/61), FA Vase Finalists (2011/12, 2013/14)

Northern League Division 2 Champions (1990/91),

Best performance in FA Cup - 1st Round Proper in 1958/59, 1960/61 and 1998/99

The village of West Auckland had a long history of coal mining. West Auckland colliery employed hundreds of men for almost 130 years until it closed in 1967. In 1909 and 1911, the West Auckland amateur football team made up of some of these hardy coalminers, won football's first World Cup. They represented the English FA in the Sir Thomas Lipton Trophy - a club tournament in Italy – beating Juventus of Italy, Stuttgart of Germany and FC Zurich and FC Winterthur of Switzerland over the 2 tournaments. The trips contributed to severe financial problems for the amateur club and they folded in 1912, reforming 2 years later as West Auckland Town FC.

The current team plays at the Wanted Stadium. The sign next to the turnstiles has the name of the stadium in large cowboy style Wanted Poster lettering (Disclaimer - Wanted Metal Recycling Limited are the stadium sponsors and I am in no way suggesting that this is a cowboy business).

Anita and I took our seats in the stand with a non-league standard Styrofoam cup of tea each. It was a nice sunny afternoon and there was a good atmosphere in the ground with a decent sized crowd of 474 for this local Auckland derby (West's opponents today were local rivals Bishop Auckland). The visitors made the brighter start and had two good chances to score early on, but it was West that took the lead after 8 minutes – a header from Amar Purewal. Bishop equalised on 20 minutes through Chris Winn and it remained all square at half time. The first half had been exciting and even. The second half was more typical derby fayre - a bit scrappy, both sides having chances to win it, both keepers making some good vital saves and towards the end tempers flaring a bit. A share of the spoils kept both sets of fans relatively happy.

Anita gave the ladies' toilets at the Wanted Stadium the unwanted accolade of the worst public toilets she had ever been in, apart from some portable toilets she remembered from Day 3 of a music festival. The quote of the day came from Bishop Auckland manager Ian Chandler to his assistant about one of their players 'He cannot pass the ball for f***ing monkey nuts'.

Vital Statistics:

West Auckland Town 1 (Purewal 8) Bishop Auckland 1 (Winn 20)

Northern League Division 1

Admission - £6

Programme – £1

Attendance – 474

RYHOPE AND GLORY

Northern League Ground 6

Tuesday 25th September 2018
RYHOPE COLLIERY WELFARE
Recreation Ground, Ryhope Street, Ryhope, Sunderland

Founded in 1892. Nickname is The Colliery Welfare. Wearside League Champions (1927/28, 1961/62, 1962/63, 1963/64, 1965/66, 2010/11, 2011/12). Promoted to the Northern League for first time at end of 2011/12 season, finished runners up in Northern League Division 2 in 2012/13, but due to ground grading issues were not promoted and relegated back to the Wearside League. Wearside League runners up in 2013/14 and promoted back to Northern League. Northern League Division 2 runners up in 2015/16 and promoted to Division 1.

Durham Challenge Cup winners (1977/78)

Best performance in FA Cup – 1st Round Proper (1967/68)

I am sure most people would think watching non-league football on a cold and windy Tuesday evening was not the ideal way to celebrate a special event, but that is what Anita and I did on our sixth wedding anniversary. We also had a pre-match happy hour cheap and cheerful not quite Michelin Star meal, but even this did not matter as we had been to a restaurant in Paris a few months earlier anyway. This was our second Northern League derby in four days – the Ryhope derby.

Ryhope Colliery Welfare (RCW) were formed by the coal miners of Ryhope in 1892 but it is only fairly recently (2016) that they reached the top division of the Northern League. They had never beaten Sunderland RCA, their near neighbours.

RCW's ground is fairly basic with the only covered seating area being a small stand behind one of the goals. Given the weather conditions, we watched the first half here, having a very good view of RCA's opener after only 2 minutes - Dom Moan firing into the roof of the net from 10 yards. We did not have such a good view of the three goals RCW scored in the first half at the other end – Craig Ellison's equaliser on 8 minutes, James Ellis' penalty on 26 minutes (RCA's Luke Page was sent off for a hand ball on the line that lead to the penalty) and Ellis' second goal on 30 minutes.

For the second half we decided to move closer to the action and stood on the half way line open to the elements. Despite being a man down, RCA had the better of the second half but for all their good build up play they did not seriously trouble Joe Atkinson in the RCW goal. The RCW defence was resolute, and overall the home side deserved their first ever Ryhope derby win.

My main concern tonight was that I may have set a high benchmark with this wedding anniversary celebration and Anita might want me to take her to Crook Town or even Tow Law next year.

Vital Statistics:

Ryhope CW 3 (Ellison 8, Ellis 26 pen, 30) Sunderland RCA 1 (Moan 2)
Northern League Division 1
Admission - £6
Programme – £1
Attendance – 180
……MISSION…..ON TRACK……..

Saturday 29th September 2018
Gateshead versus Eastleigh
Gateshead International Stadium

With a very early flight to Mallorca to catch on Sunday 30th September, I decided against travelling to a Northern League ground today. I took the opportunity instead to make the short drive from home to the GIS to watch The Heed for only the second time this season.

I sat with my friend Ken Richardson as I have been doing during the last 10 years of watching Gateshead – ever since Anita and I sat near him at a match when he was wearing a full length sheepskin coat and decided he would be a person worth getting to know. Ken is a man of many talents. A useful goalkeeper in his day (or so he tells me), a former schoolteacher well respected by his former pupils (or so an ex-work colleague of mine and ex-pupil of his tells me), now retired, heavily involved in amateur dramatics and TV extra work, sang Abide With Me on the Wembley turf at the 2015 FA Cup Final with Alfie Boe and the FA Cup Fans Choir (he was Gateshead FC's representative), also an Elvis impersonator and has appeared on stage with The Darkness at the Hammersmith Odeon as his alter ego of The Butler. He is also one of the most vocal of Gateshead's supporters, with a particular interest in telling the referee and linesmen when he feels they have made an error.

It is fair to say that Steve Watson's young Gateshead side have exceeded expectations so far this season but today was to ultimately prove frustrating and disappointing. There was not much goalmouth action in the first half – Eastleigh defended well as The Heed huffed and puffed but did not really create much. Gateshead looked more dangerous after the break. They had a strong claim for a penalty turned down on 53 minutes and Robbie Tinkler (who had recently been included in the England C squad) hit the bar on 72 minutes then hit the post on 74 minutes. Eastleigh then scored on 77 minutes – Josh Hare's strike from outside the box being their only shot on target during the whole match.

After this disappointing defeat, Ken told me that it may be better if I stay away from the GIS and continue going to Northern League matches instead.

Vital Statistics:

Gateshead 0 Eastleigh 1 (Hare 77)
National League
Admission - £10 (club recently reduced adult charge from £15)
Programme – didn't buy one
Attendance – 655 (15 away fans)

The next day Anita and I thankfully got up in time to catch our early flight from Newcastle Airport to Palma, Mallorca. We were staying at Puerto de Pollenca on the north of the island for 5 nights, and I was hoping to attend a match while I was there. The local team play in the Primera Regional Mallorca Liga and were scheduled to play Baleares Sin Fronteras at home on the weekend of 29/30 September. A few weeks earlier I checked the league's website (ffib.es) and it listed the match as taking place on Sunday 30th September kick off time TBA. Given that we would arrive in Puerto de Pollenca around midday and the matches generally kick off in the late afternoon or early evening, it looked possible I would eventually be able to attend a Puerto de Pollenca FC match (we have been to this holiday location a number of times in the past 8 years and for various reasons I had never seen them play). Imagine my disappointment when I checked the website a week before we went to find the kick off time was now confirmed as 6.30 pm.... on Saturday 29th September! 'C'est la vie' as they say in France....or 'Asi es la vida' as they say in Spain. We walked up to the ground on Tuesday afternoon, I took a few photos, and gradually got over my disappointment of what would have been a great Spanish ground tick. For the record Puerto de Pollenca FC won the match 4-1.

FRIDAY NIGHT THRILLER
Northern League Ground 7

Friday 26th October 2018
WHICKHAM
Glebe Sports Ground, Rectory Lane, Whickham, Tyne and Wear

Formed in 1944 as Axwell Park Colliery Welfare (colloquially known as The Home Guard Team) and played in the Derwent Valley League. Joined Wearside League in 1974, champions in 1977/78 and 1987/88. Promoted to Northern League Division 2 for 1988/89 season, finished 3rd and promoted to Division 1. Relegated back to Division 2 in 1991/92, promoted again as Division 2 Champions in 1994/95, but relegated again in 1996/97. Promoted again to Division 1 in 2017/18. Nicknamed The Lang Jacks.

FA Vase winners (1980/81)

Durham Challenge Cup winners (2005/06)

Best performance in FA Cup – 2nd Qualifying Round in 1995/96 and 2003/04

Another Newcastle Benfield away match with Kev saw us head to the suburban town of Whickham in the Borough of Gateshead. Before this Friday evening kick off, we had a couple of pints in their clubhouse. The tracksuited Whickham team were also in there, but it was good to see they were not drinking alcohol. We spoke to one of those typical groundhopping types who Kev knew - a man with a jacket full of club pin badges, from all levels of the English football pyramid. It was pretty impressive and made me realise what a novice I really am at this groundhopping game.

This was Whickham's first season back in the top division after 20 years in Northern League Division 2 and they were finding it a bit tough going so far, currently lying in 2nd bottom place.

With hats and scarfs on to combat a cold and windy night, we stood on the sidelines with Keith, a Benfield fan who Kev introduced to me as a serial abuser of linesmen – and it did not take long for him to live up to that reputation. He was not the only person abusing the linesman though on this side of the pitch. Midway through the first half, one of Whickham's coaching staff ran 20 yards out of their dugout to give the linesman some verbals. The referee sent the coach off to the stand. He still managed to shout loud enough to be heard now and again from the stand though – quite an achievement!

The match was a 6 goal thriller. Whickham took the lead on 18 minutes – Andrew Bulford slotting the ball home from a tight angle with Benfield keeper Andrew Grainger way off his line. The visitors levelled soon after via a Paul Brayson tap in and took the lead on the half hour mark – a good finish from Jake Orrell. It stayed 2-1 to Benfield at the half time break but it could have been more – Brayson and Scott McCarthy missing good chances.

Bulford's second goal brought the home side level on 78 minutes. Benfield substitute Dale Pearson restored their lead on 85 minutes and they looked to be heading for a victory when Whickham went down to 10 men after Steven Little was dismissed with only a few minutes of added time remaining. However, in the 96th minute Bulford completed his hat-trick to give Whickham a vital point.

Vital Statistics:

Whickham 3 (Bulford 18, 78, 96)
Newcastle Benfield 3 (Brayson 25, Orrell 32, Pearson 85)
Northern League Division 1
Admission - £6
Programme – £1
Attendance – 144

A TRIP TO THE MORGUE
Northern League Ground 8

Saturday 27th October 2018
NORTH SHIELDS
Daren Persson Stadium, 38 West Percy Road, North Shields, Tyne and Wear

Formed in 1896 as North Shields Athletic and played in the South Shields and District League, then the Northern Combination League, Northern Alliance and North Eastern League until the outbreak of the First World War in 1914. After WW1 they re-emerged as Preston Colliery, playing in the 1919/20 Tyneside League, then the Northern Alliance and North Eastern League again. Became North Shields FC for 1928/29 season in the North Eastern League and played in that league until it disbanded in 1958. Joined the Midland League, then Northern Counties League. They joined the Northern League in the 1964/65 season and played in it until 1989. Changes in the non-league pyramid structure and financial difficulties saw the club drop to the Wearside League in 1992. Re-joined the Northern League Division 2 in 2012 and were promoted to Division 1 as champions in 2013/14. Nicknamed The Robins.

FA Vase winners (2014/15)

FA Amateur Cup winners (1968/69),

European Amateur Cup winners (1968/69)

Northern League Division 1 champions (1968/69)

Northern League Cup winners (1968/69, 1971/72)

Northumberland Senior Cup winners 13 times, most recently in 2016

The following day I attended this match with Mark, a Toon supporter friend (one of the Frankfurt/Pink Trick crowd from Chapter 3) who like me had become gradually more and more disillusioned with the Mike Ashley era at Newcastle United, and was now up for giving this non-league football a bash.

The day started with heavy rain and cold strong winds but the weather had brightened up a bit at the coast when we arrived at the Daren Persson Stadium (it is named after the club's main sponsor - a local funeral director – and is nicknamed The Morgue) for North Shields match with West Auckland.

We had a couple of pre-match pints in the very well-furnished clubhouse and walked around to the covered seating area, past a few North Shields Ultras (who bizarrely have their own advertising board in a corner of the ground), who were actually not too scary. One accidently bumped into me and apologised – hardly the normal behaviour of a Football Club Ultra. I assumed this must be the friendly non-league variety of Ultra.

West Auckland went into this match on a run of 6 games without a win, but they ended that today with 2 well taken second half goals by Amar Purewal. Both sides played the game in a positive manner in chilly conditions. Overall I felt West deserved their win, particularly based on their second half performance where they controlled the tempo better than the home side. Gary Day pulled a goal back for the Robins with 12 minutes to go but West held out to claim the 3 points.

Vital Statistics:

North Shields 1 (Day 78) West Auckland Town 2 (Purewal 50, 67)

Northern League Division 1

Admission - £6

Programme – £1.50

Attendance – 201

AT THE HOME OF TWO WORLD CUP WINNERS
Northern League Ground 9

Saturday 10th November 2018
ASHINGTON
Woodhorn Lane, Ashington, Northumberland

Formed in 1883 as Ashington Rising Star. Joined the Northern Alliance in 1892/93 season, then played in East Northumberland League and North Eastern League.

Elected to Third Division North of the Football League in 1921 but after finishing bottom of the league in 1928/29 season they dropped back into the North Eastern League. After playing in the Midland League, Northern Counties League, Wearside League and North Regional League, they became a founder member of the Northern Premier League in 1968. Joined the Northern League in 1970. Nicknamed The Colliers given the town's proud mining history.

Northern League Division 2 champions (2000/01, 2003/04),

Northumberland Senior Cup winners 10 times, most recently in 2013.

Best performance in FA Cup – 3rd Round Proper in 1926/27.

Two weeks later Anita and I drove to Ashington in Northumberland. On arriving at this former coal mining town, our first stop was a visit to Beatrice Street, where the Charlton brothers (Bobby and the late Jack) grew up in the 1940s. We walked along this street of modest terraced houses and then down its back lane, where Bobby and Jack learnt to play football by spending endless hours kicking a ball around. It was similar to the Gateshead back lane that my brother and I used to play football in when we were young. We of course did not go on to play in a World Cup winning team like the two brothers who played football in this Ashington back lane. Jack had a brief spell working down the mine but it is fair to say that being good at football saved the Charlton brothers from the working life that many of their childhood friends would endure underground. It felt like we were looking at a place that was just as historic as the Colosseum in Rome or the Pyramids in Egypt.

Next stop was the Woodhorn Lane ground. The sign in the car park proclaims Ashington Community Football Club and we were certainly greeted with a very friendly welcome from the man taking the gate money and selling programmes. We had a cup of tea in the very well-appointed clubhouse located behind the very well-appointed main stand. There have been some questions as to whether there was an appropriate use of public money to help fund the building of this stand and clubhouse but it is without doubt an impressive set up for this level of football.

This weekend was the 100th anniversary of the end of the First World War. It is estimated that around 20 million men lost their lives in battle during the conflict, with an estimated similar number of wounded. Hundreds of footballers, both professional and amateur, were killed in action after being called up to fight following the suspension of competitive football in Britain for 4 years during the hostilities. Before the kick-off a trumpeter played 'The Last Post' followed by 2 minutes silence that was impeccably observed by the crowd.

After exiting 3 cup competitions in the last 2 weeks, the home side's poor run continued against Newton Aycliffe today. The visitors were having a lot of joy down the right wing in the first half and Ashington's midfield look inept. 3 goals from Aycliffe in a 13 minute first half spell effectively killed the game off. They had a few chances to further increase their lead in the second half, but in the end they settled for and deserved their 3-0 win, which lifted them above Ashington in the Northern League Division 1 table.

Vital Statistics:

Ashington 0 Newton Aycliffe 3 (Wood 28, Gavin 30, Gash 41)

Northern League Division 1

Admission - £6

Programme – £1

Attendance – 199

.......MISSION......AT HALFWAY STAGE.......

RED STAR BLUES
Northern League Ground 10

Saturday 17th November 2018
SEAHAM RED STAR
The Ferguson Motor Repairs Stadium, Seaham Town Park,
Stockton Road, Seaham, Co Durham

Formed in 1973 in the Red Star pub and played in the Houghton and District League. Joined the Northern Alliance in 1974, then the Wearside League in 1979 and Northern League Division 2 in 1983. Promoted to Northern League Division 1 in 1987/88. Relegated back to Division 2 in 2001/02, promoted to Division 1 in 2006/07, relegated again in 2010/11, then promoted again in 2014/15. Nicknamed The Star.

Best league performance – Runners-up in Northern League Division 1 (1999/2000).

Northern League Division 2 champions (2014/15)

Northern League Cup winners (1992/93),

Durham Challenge Cup winners (1978/79)

Aweek later, Anita accompanied me again, this time to the seaside town of Seaham. Before the match we stopped off at the seafront to view the impressive large rusty red steel statue of a First World War soldier by artist/sculptor Ray Lonsdale, which is commonly known as 'Tommy'. We also located the recently added commemorative permanent metal poppy for Anita's great uncle (who was born in Seaham and killed in action in the First World War) from the display on the railings overlooking the North Sea near to the town's war memorial.

We then drove to the stadium at Seaham Town Park and took our seats in the main stand on what was a chilly November afternoon for The Star's clash with Ryhope CW.

Seaham Red Star have had a poor start to the season but they have improved recently and were on an unbeaten 3 match run going into today's game. They had a nightmare start today though, going behind to a Jack Devlin goal after four minutes. Ryhope looked the better side in the first half but could not add to their early lead. Against the run of play, the home side equalised when Michael Chilton fired the ball into the roof of the net on 38 minutes. Things went from bad to worse for the visitors when Danni Lay was sent off at the end of the first-half for a second bookable foul, and the teams went off at half time all square.

Seaham started strongly after the break but they were also reduced to 10 men on the hour mark when Anthony Myers collided with Ryhope's Robbie Bird in the penalty area. Matthew Weirs coolly converted the penalty. Nathaniel Skidmore made it 3-1 to Ryhope on 75 minutes. The visitors closed out the match efficiently and should have scored more, Rae and Bird missing late chances.

Vital Statistics:

Seaham Red Star 1 (Chilton 38)

Ryhope CW 3 (Devlin 4, Weirs 60 pen, Skidmore 75)

Northern League Division 1

Admission - £6

Programme – £1

Attendance – 65

Sunday 2nd December 2018
Berliner Fussballclub Dynamo versus VfB Auerbach 1906
Friedrich-Ludwig-Jahn Sportpark, Prenzlauer Berg, Berlin, Germany

When Anita and I had a 4 day European city break to Berlin in early December, it presented a good challenge for me to test how serious a groundhopper I had now become. We planned to take in the Christmas markets, various museums and other attractions – and I wanted to go to a football match if at all possible. Unfortunately, Bundesliga side Hertha Berlin were playing away, and Bundesliga 2 side FC Union Berlin were playing at home a few hours before we arrived on Saturday 1st December. The only reasonable option was to go to watch Berliner FC Dynamo on Sunday 2nd December.

As previously recalled in Chapter 3, in 2006 I went to a Newcastle United Europa League match in Germany with some friends at Eintracht Frankfurt's Commerzbank Arena. It was an unremarkable match but a great atmosphere. It would have been great to savour the exciting atmosphere of top level German football again. Hertha have average crowds of over 50,000 and Union have average crowds of around 20,000 but it was not to be, with Dynamo usually only attracting in the region of 500 fans in the Fourth Tier of German football (English League Two level). Nevertheless, we were very much looking forward to the experience as we boarded the U-Bahn train at Alexanderplatz (the station near our hotel) for the short 3 stop journey to Eberswalder Strasse station near to Dynamo's ground at the Friedrich-Ludwig-Jahn Sportpark.

The stadium is located in what was formerly East Berlin and the club had strong links with the Stasi (the East German state security service). The Berlin Wall and the notorious Death Strip ran right behind the ground, separating it from West Berlin. At about 12.15 we arrived at the entrance, where there were a few Polizei but not many fans. I only then realised that the kick off time was actually 1.30 not 12.30 (I forgot about the hour long time difference between GMT in the UK and Germany - schoolboy error) so we trotted off to a nearby coffee shop.

Back outside the stadium for the correct kick off time, we bought 2 tickets from the concrete container type ticket office. My ticket cost 12 euros but Anita's only cost 8 euros because she is a woman. I understand this sometimes happens at grounds in mainland Europe. At the entrance we were both vigorously body searched by stewards, then in complete contrast, a youngster gave us a chocolate Santa each (he later bizarrely appeared in the stand near to us wearing a black shirt with 'Security' written on the back). The overall capacity of the stadium is 19,708 with very colourful alternating rows of red, yellow and blue seats stretching all around the pitch that also has an athletics track around it (reminded me of The GIS). We took our seats in the main stand but decided to move when some Ultras with large flags stood in the rows in front of us. We moved to the other end of the stand, sitting beside a group of chain smokers instead (it seemed the lesser of two evils).

The match kicked off and it did take long for the home fans to start grumbling when Zimmermann opened the scoring for Auerbach after only 4 minutes. Dynamo looked the better side after this but it was the visitors who missed a glorious chance to double their lead after 20 minutes. The home side had two players booked in a minute on 25 minutes, and they had a few good chances to equalise but the Auerbach keeper made some good saves to deny them. Against the run of play on 37 minutes the visitors made it 2-0. At half time we had a cup of gluhwein to warm us up a bit.

The match was effectively settled as a contest when Zimmermann scored his second goal on the hour mark. Even though the home fans were clearly unhappy, there was still some good natured chanting and general banter going on. Anita even tried to start a new chant of 'Go Go Dynamo' - without success. We particularly enjoyed the clapping that went on during a Dynamo player's run up to take a corner (similar to an athletics crowd clapping a long jumper's run up). Towards the end of the second half we had a good chat with a Hertha Berlin season ticket holder who was sitting in the row in front of us. He wanted to keep it quiet that he was attending this match – his first time at Dynamo. It almost felt like the Stasi were still operating here.

All in all it was an enjoyable experience and a decent match where Auerbach took their chances and Dynamo did not. This was a great first day of our European city break - for the other 3 days I changed from groundhopper to tourist.

Vital Statistics:

BFC Dynamo 0 VfB Auerbach 3 (Zimmermann 4, 60, Schlosser 37)
German Regionalliga Nordost
Admission – 12 euros or 8 euros depending on your gender
Programme – 2 euros
Gluhwein – 2.5 euros
Attendance – 301

CHAPTER

COMPLETING DIVISION 1

AROUND THE NORTHERN LEAGUE GROUNDS

(Part 2 – December 2018 to March 2019)

Just as many birds change to a winter plumage with the arrival of the colder weather, the groundhopper will put on warmer clothing in the winter months. This will be required for survival when sitting or standing at a match anywhere in the UK (but from personal experience Scotland in particular). A thick coat, scarf, wool hat, gloves, thick socks, long johns (for the men) and woolly tights (for the ladies) should all be considered essential for Saturday afternoons (when the temperature from half time onwards regularly drops dramatically) or Tuesday/ Wednesday evenings (when it is usually freezing even before the match kicks off).

Extra clothing was certainly required for most of the winter stage of The Mission....

......MISSION.....GOOD PROGRESS, REMAIN FOCUSSED....

ARTIFICIAL INTELLIGENCE
Northern League Ground 11

Saturday 8th December 2018
CONSETT
The Belle View Stadium, Delves Lane, Consett

Formed in 1899 as Consett Celtic. Joined the Northern Alliance in 1919 and changed name to Consett FC in 1922. Also played in North Eastern League, Midland League, Northern Counties League and Wearside League. Joined the Northern League in 1970. Nicknamed The Steelmen given the town's former steel making history.

Northern League Division 2 champions (1988/89, 2005/06)

Northern League Cup winners (1994/95)

Durham Challenge Cup winners (1947/48, 1949/50, 1958/59, 1960/61, 1968/69, 2006/07, 2017/18)

Best FA Cup performance – 1st Round Proper in 1958/59 and 1996/97.

On a very cold December day, I could not find anyone to accompany me to another Northern League ground tick, so I did a flying solo trip to the former steelworks town of Consett in County Durham. I drove there and whilst it was sunny and reasonably mild when I set off from home, when I arrived half an hour later at the more elevated location of Consett it was a different kettle of fish. It was raining heavily with a very cold wind blowing (although it is said that this type of weather can regularly occur in July up here never mind in December). In the 2012/13 season, Consett had 18 home games postponed at their previous ground in the town due to the harsh weather. They moved nearby to the newly built Belle View Stadium in 2013. An artificial 3G pitch was installed at the ground to minimise postponements and it has worked (a good example of a different kind of Artificial Intelligence!). The stadium looks impressive with a well-appointed clubhouse and refreshments area and two small stands with fold down seats on each side of the pitch. I bought a cup of tea and took my seat in the stand next to the dugouts.

Thankfully the rain stopped just before kick-off and stayed away for most of the match, apart from brief downpour in the second half. Consett went into today's match in 2nd place in Division 1 with visitors Ashington struggling in 14th place. Ashington's performances have improved of late though and they matched their hosts in the first half. Each side had a few chances but some good goalkeeping kept it goalless at the interval.

For the second half I moved to the other side of the pitch and stood on the touchline. It was now absolutely freezing and when the rain started around the hour mark I took refuge in the stand. Soon after this, Ashington had a decent shout for a goal denied, the referee ruling that the ball had not crossed the line (no VAR at this level of course). On 72 minutes Ashington's resolute defence was breached when Matty Slocombe headed home the rebound after Danny Craggs' 25 yard free kick hit the angle of the post and crossbar. Five minutes later a Michael Sweet penalty made it 2-0 to clinch the win for the home team. I felt the 2 goal margin flattered Consett today, with Ashington producing a greatly improved performance compared to when Anita and I watched them at Woodhorn Lane in November.

At the final whistle I wasted no time in driving back home, with the heater in the car on full blast, to thaw out.

Vital Statistics:

Consett 2 (Slocombe 72, Sweet 77 pen) Ashington 0
Northern League Division 1
Admission - £6
Programme – £1.50
Attendance – 361

Wednesday 26th December 2018
Gateshead versus Hartlepool United
Gateshead International Stadium

For the second season running, Gateshead's Boxing Day fixture was a home match against Hartlepool, geographically their closest National League rivals after 'Pools were relegated from the Football League at the end of the 2016/17 season. I was looking forward to watching The Heed in action for the first time in almost 3 months.

I drove to the GIS in good time for the kick off. As expected there was a larger than normal crowd and I took my seat in Ken and I's usual area of the Tyne and Wear Stand. The match kicked off with no sign of Ken and after ten minutes I assumed that, although he very rarely misses a Heed home game, Christmas family commitments must be preventing him from attending. However, after ten minutes, I heard him shouting loudly at the ref from a few rows back, so normal service was restored!

Gateshead had not conceded a goal in their previous four home games and started brightly today. After ten minutes Luke Armstrong headed just over the bar, and three minutes later he opened the scoring with a strong low shot that crept under the 'Pools keeper. On 20 minutes Robbie Tinkler was unlucky not to double Gateshead's lead when his 35 yard strike hit the bar. The Heed did make it 2-0 on 33 minutes, Armstrong tapping home Scott Barrow's deflected shot. The home side were good value for their two goal lead at half time.

Hartlepool improved after the break and both sides had half chances to add to the scoring. The Heed looked like seeing out a deserved win but there was to be some late drama and a very nervy ending to the match. Gateshead were reduced to 10 men after 84 minutes when Tom White was dismissed for a challenge on Josh Hawkes on the halfway line. Two minutes later Liam Noble converted a penalty for Hartlepool to make it 2-1. 'Pools were then awarded another penalty on 89 minutes. Noble again sent Heed keeper Aynsley Pears the wrong way but this time his spot kick hit the outside of the post and went behind. 5 minutes of additional time saw Hartlepool pressing for the equaliser (they hit the bar) and The Heed hanging on. It was a great relief when the referee blew the final whistle.

I caught up with Ken at the end of the match and overall we thought The Heed deservedly survived the late scare to record another good win and remain in the National League play off places. This win meant that after being the bookies' favourites to finish bottom of the National League at the start of the season, Gateshead now only needed 5 points from their remaining 20 games to be safe from relegation.

Vital Statistics:

Gateshead 2 (Armstrong 13, 33) Hartlepool 1 (Noble 87 pen)
National League
Admission - £16.50 (£15 + £1.50 'scandalous' booking fee)
Programme – didn't buy one
Attendance – 2,678 (1,477 away fans)

ON THE BUS WITH THE BENFIELD FANS
Northern League Ground 12

Saturday 29th December 2018
GUISBOROUGH TOWN
King George V Ground, Howlbeck Road, Guisborough, North Yorkshire

Formed in 1973 and played in the Middlesbrough and District League. Also played in the South Bank and District League, Northern Alliance, Midland League and Northern Counties East League. Joined the Northern League in 1985. Nicknamed The Priorymen

Northern League Division 2 runners-up (1986/87, 2010/11)

Northern League Cup winners (1988/89),

North Riding Senior Cup winners (1989/90, 1990/91, 1992/93, 1993/94, 2010/11, 2013/14).

Best FA Cup performance – 1st Round Proper (1988/89).

Best FA Vase performance – Finalists (1979/80).

Kev Larkham was by now a firm Newcastle Benfield fan (he had hardly missed a match so far this season home or away) and he asked me if I fancied travelling with him on the Benfield Supporters Club' minibus for their match away to Guisborough. It was a lovely December day and given that it was one of the longest journeys of The Mission I took up the offer. We met up with the other 6 hardy travelling Benfield supporters at the Powder Monkey pub in Wallsend at 1 pm. After the obligatory group photo in the car park holding the club flag, and fortified by Greggs' sausage rolls, we set off for North Yorkshire.

We arrived at the scenic KGV Ground shortly after 2 pm for a pre-match pint in the well-appointed social club (that rather bizarrely was officially opened by TV presenter / journalist Selina Scott in 1983). Kev and I stood with the other Benfield fans in the covered standing enclosure on the opposite side of the pitch to the main stand and dugouts. The rating of the Benfield fans touchline banter with the linesman throughout the match would have to be Certificate 18, Warning Explicit Content, and Parental Guidance Required. Kev had been providing the Twitter goal and incident updates on Benfield's matches since mid-November and he was on duty again. He explained to me that it was a huge responsibility when thousands of people are waiting on your every word. I noticed that his tongue was firmly in his cheek as he said this, but on a serious note, good quality updates on social media from games as the action happens can only help to bring non-league football to a wider audience.

Benfield started brightly, with Paul Brayson and Dale Pearson forcing saves from Guisborough's keeper Jordan Nixon within the first quarter of an hour. The home side then had a good spell and took the lead on 20 minutes when Mason McNeill smashed a loose ball into the roof of the net. The Priorymen finished the first half strongly and I felt they just shaded it overall.

It was a different story in the second half. Benfield laid siege on the Guisborough goal and on the hour mark Dean Holmes scored his first goal for the club, heading home Jake Orrell's cross. The visitors took a 2-1 lead on 75 minutes – Brayson controlling the ball from his keeper Andy Grainger's goal kick and calmly steering it over Nixon. Benfield were by far the better side in the second half and held on to their lead to take their unbeaten run to 14 games.

The minibus headed back up the A19 shortly after 5 pm. It had been a really good day – unseasonably mild weather, good craic, a great little ground with friendly supporters and a very entertaining game of football.

Vital Statistics:

Guisborough 1 (McNeill 20) Newcastle Benfield 2 (Holmes 60, Brayson 75)
Northern League Division 1
Admission - £6
Programme – £1.50
Attendance – 159

BISHOPS' SECOND HALF SUCCESS
Northern League Ground 13

Wednesday 9th January 2019
BISHOP AUCKLAND
Heritage Park. Stadium Way, Bishop Auckland, County Durham

Formed in 1882 as Bishop Auckland Church Institute by theological students from Oxford and Cambridge Universities whilst studying at Auckland Castle. After a dispute, a breakaway team Auckland Town became founder members of the Northern League in 1889, then became Bishop Auckland in 1893. Between 1893 and 1988 the club won the Northern League a record 19 times. Joined the Northern Premier League in 1988 (runners up in 1988/89 and 1996/97). Re-joined the Northern League in 2006.

FA Amateur Cup winners 10 times most recently in 1956/57

Durham Challenge Cup winners 16 times most recently in 2012/13.

Northern League Cup winners 8 times most recently in 1975/76.

Best FA Cup performance 4th Round (1954/55).

Best FA Trophy performance Quarter Final (1978/79, 1996/97, 1999/2000)

For the first Northern League ground visit of 2019, Anita and I went to Bishop Auckland for their match with Newton Aycliffe. After a pre-match meal at the Stanley Jefferson (aka Stan Laurel) Wetherspoons pub in the town, we headed to Heritage Park, Bishops' fairly new ground (built 2010) and took our seats behind the dugouts in the very pleasant main stand. At the side of the stand there are some bricks with names of players and fans inscribed on them. One of them had Duncan Edwards name on it, and Anita said she did not realise he had played for Bishop Auckland. He had not of course, but the connection is that after the Munich air crash in 1958 Bishop Auckland loaned 3 players to Manchester United to enable them to fulfil their fixtures after 8 of their players including the great Duncan Edwards lost their lives in the disaster.

Bishops would move up to second in the table with a draw or a win tonight, and they started brightly. However, it was a well organised Aycliffe side that opened the scoring on 25 minutes – Vincent Nash running onto a long ball and neatly slotting a low shot into the bottom corner of the net past Bishops' keeper Nick Liversedge. Aycliffe doubled their lead on 34 minutes - Nash scoring his second with another low shot into the bottom corner that this time passed through a crowd of players in the penalty area. The visitors comfortably held onto their 2 goal lead at half time and the home fans around us were not at all happy with the first half showing from Bishops.

As the second half kicked off, the home players looked like they had received a rocket during the interval (Manager Ian Chandler later wrote on Twitter that some words of encouragement and direction were given at half time). They quickly reduced the deficit on 47 minutes via a Chris Winn header. On 53 minutes, a late challenge by Bishops' Callum Munro on Nash earned him a yellow card, and Nash's retaliation to the challenge right in front of the referee earned him a red card.

With the man advantage, Bishops were now looking like a side worthy of their high league position but a resilient Aycliffe were proving hard to break down. The home side's pressure eventually told on 74 minutes when Munro equalised after a goalmouth scramble. After the equaliser, the Bishops' fan sitting in front of us sent a torrent of swearwords in the direction of Aycliffe's manager Deano Browne in the nearby technical area (Alanis Morissette would certainly describe this as ironic given that when Deano had used some bad language in the first half this same fan had told him it was not tolerated at Heritage Park!).

On 84 minutes Aycliffe were awarded a free kick on the edge of the box and brought on substitute Tom Gavin – their free kick specialist - to take it. His kick sailed high over the bar. A few minutes later he was then taken off again! All of 10-man Aycliffe's efforts were undone after 86 minutes when Andrew Johnson headed Bishops into a 3-2 lead. The home side held on for a vital win but we were impressed with Aycliffe's fighting spirit and felt they deserved something from tonight's very entertaining encounter on a cold January evening.

The drive back on the A688 and A1 was mainly characterised by Anita whingeing on about how cold she was – luckily it was a smooth journey with no delays and we were back home by 10.30 pm.

Vital Statistics:

Bishop Auckland 3 (Winn 47, Munro 74, Johnson 86)

Newton Aycliffe 2 (Nash 25, 34)

Northern League Division 1

Admission - £6

Programme – £1

Attendance – 309

AYCLIFFE OUTCLASSED
Northern League Ground 14

Saturday 19th January 2019
NEWTON AYCLIFFE
Newton Aycliffe Stadium, Moore Lane, Newton Aycliffe, County Durham

Generally accepted as forming in 1985 (previously linked clubs were Newton Aycliffe Rangers in 1951, Newton Rangers, and Newton Aycliffe Sports Club in 1969). Played in the Wearside League until folding in 1994. Re-formed and played in Durham Alliance then Wearside League again. Promoted to Northern League Division 2 in 2009. Northern League Division 2 champions in 2010/11 season and promoted to Division 1.

Highest finish in Northern League Division 1 – 6th in 2015/16 season.

Durham Challenge Cup winners (2015/16)

Best performance in FA Vase – 5th Round Last 16 (2015/16)

Anita and I had planned to go to this match several weeks earlier, but as it got nearer the wintry weather was starting to take hold a bit in the North East. Ice and snow had initially been forecast for the Newton Aycliffe area, potentially putting the game in doubt, but it turned out to be not so serious and by mid-morning on match day it was confirmed to be on. After the Dynamo Berlin match we attended in early December, Anita had said that, like the Bundesliga and a number of other European leagues, she was taking a winter break. She reneged on this at Bishop Auckland last week and she braved the elements with her thermals on again today for Aycliffe's clash with high flying Dunston.

We took our seats in the William Finley Stand that is located on the opposite side of the pitch to the dugouts. Only 10 days ago at Bishop Auckland, Anita had dubbed Aycliffe's dreadlocked manager Deano Browne her favourite Northern League manager, but they parted company with him days before today's match, so as Anita looked over at the dugouts there was no love interest for her (she had to settle for me again).

The hosts started well but Dunston soon showed why they are challenging for the league title. They are a well organised physical side with some skilful tricky players. They opened the scoring after 17 minutes when Scott Heslop passed to the unmarked Mark Fitzpatrick who slotted it home. Aycliffe's Joshua Rodgers was sent off on 23 minutes, considered by the ref to have denied a goal scoring opportunity.

It looked debatable to us and the red card seemed a bit harsh given that the ref was about 20 yards behind play. It certainly made an already difficult task even harder for Aycliffe. Dunston's second goal on 36 minutes was a beauty, Jack Elliott coolly finishing into the bottom corner after a mazy run.

We had brought a flask of homemade soup with us (as we were now proper non-league football fans) and we had some at half time to warm us up a bit. The second half saw Dunston in control and Jordan Nellis made it 3-0 on 69 minutes. The home side never gave up though, and on 75 minutes pulled one back, Marc Costello scoring with a header from Ethan Wood's cross. However, two late goals from Mark Fitzpatrick made sure of the victory and completed his hat trick. We moved from the stand for the last few minutes and stood behind the Dunston goal. This provided a great view of Aycliffe's second goal on 88 minutes, Stuart Thompson slotting the ball past the keeper from close range after a good passing move.

This win, and Consett's draw with Whitley Bay, meant Dunston leap frogged them to the top of the table. As we headed back north on the A1 we listened to BBC Radio Newcastle, where Newcastle and Sunderland fans were phoning in with their usual post-match views. The Toon had beaten Cardiff 3-0 at St James Park and some of the phone-in fans were celebrating like they had won the League rather than still languishing in the relegation zone. A late Scunthorpe equaliser had denied Sunderland a win at Glandford Park. This is not a good combination for Anita and a far cry from Sunderland's 4-1 wins when she attended some previous Northern League matches.

Vital Statistics:

Newton Aycliffe 2 (Costello 75, Thompson 88)
Dunston UTS 5 (Fitzpatrick 17, 84, 86, Elliott 36, Nellis 69)
Northern League Division 1
Admission - £6, Programme – £1
Attendance – 110

AT THE GROUND NEAREST TO (ARGUABLY) THE BEST PUB IN THE WORLD

Northern League Ground 15

Saturday 26th January 2019
RYTON AND CRAWCROOK ALBION
Kingsley Park, Stannerford Road, Crawcrook, Tyne and Wear

Formed in 1970 as pub team Ryton FC. Joined Northern Alliance in 1988, First Division champions 1996/97, Premier Division champions 2004/05 and promoted to Northern League Division 2. Promoted to Northern League Division 1 in 2007/08. Relegated to Division 2 in 2010/11. Changed name to Ryton and Crawcrook Albion in 2011/12.

Durham Challenge Cup runners-up (2009/10)

My companions for my first Northern League Division 2 ground tick at Ryton and Crawcrook Albion (RACA) were Derek 'Dekka' Muse and David 'Robbo' Robinson. They are both Sunderland FC season ticket holders but they occasionally enjoy watching non-league football when Sunderland are not playing at home.

We caught the 12.55 train from Newcastle Central Station for the short 20 minute journey to Wylam, and went into The Boathouse public house that is just across the road from Wylam Station. A sign at the pub door reads 'Arguably, the best pub in the world' – that is some boast, but what certainly cannot be argued about is that it is the best pub to meet for a couple of pints before a RACA match. After having a couple of pints, we walked the mile or so up the road (and uphill) to the ground, arriving ten minutes before kick-off for RACA's match against Heaton Stannington (affectionately known as The Stan).

Up to this point it was a dry but cold and windy day. Being hardy souls, we stood on the decking terrace outside of the pleasant clubhouse with more beers. It was not long before someone was approaching Dekka saying 'Hi Dek, how you doing'? Wherever I go with Dekka this always happens. For someone who is not an actual North East celebrity like say Ant and Dec or Jimmy Nail, there are certainly a hell of a lot of people who know him. Robbo commented that RACA's black and blue striped shirts and The Stan's black and white striped shirts made it look like an Inter Milan v Juventus match. Even though the Kingsley Park ground is in a very picturesque rural location, given the state of the pitch and the sparse crowd, it did not feel much like the San Siro.

RACA were without their top scorer and, it seems, fans' favourite Scott Jasper following his red card in their previous match. The Stan were the better side in the early stages but were unable to seriously trouble the RACA goal. The wind and the general state of the pitch were not making it easy for either team. It was the home side who came closest to scoring in the first half when a sweet Tyler Davis volley from the edge of the box on 22 minutes was saved low by Stan keeper Daniel Regan. It remained goalless at half time. Perhaps the slickest move of the first half was by Dekka, when towards half time it started raining and he sprinted into the clubhouse.

Robbo had noticed that Stan's Number 10 Andy Robertson was also being called Robbo by his team mates. He then started to reminisce about his football playing days – that didn't take long! Five minutes into the second half, the Robbo playing football today flicked the ball onto Connor Campbell who beat two defenders and fired the ball past RACA keeper Stefan Holden to give The Stan the lead. The rain then started to fall more heavily and the pitch was cutting up. The Stan's Robbo hit the bar on 57 minutes, but there were only another couple of half chances for each side as the conditions worsened and it finished 1-0 to the visitors.

With the rain getting heavier and the temperature dropping even further, we headed off back down the road to The Boathouse. We had only walked a few hundred yards when a kind RACA fan offered us a lift that we gratefully accepted. We were soon ensconced back in the Boathouse next to the warm fire and had another couple of pints before catching the 6.20 pm train back to Newcastle. It had not been an absolute classic of a match, but we had been to a great little ground and pub, and we all agreed it had been a great day out.

Vital Statistics:

Ryton and Crawcrook Albion 0

Heaton Stannington 1 (Campbell 49)

Northern League Division 2

Admission - £5

Programme – £1

Attendance – 42

CUP FEVER HITS HEATON
Northern League Ground 16

Wednesday 6th February 2019
HEATON STANNINGTON
Grounsell Park, Newton Road, High Heaton, Newcastle upon Tyne

Officially formed in 1910. Joined Tyneside Minor League in 1913, then Northern Amateur League in 1914. Elected to Northern League in 1939. After 5 consecutive bottom three finishes, they resigned after 1951/52 season and spent 4 seasons in the Northern Alliance. Re-joined the Northern Amateur League in 1956, then played in North Eastern League from 1959, Northern Combination League from 1960 and Wearside League from 1973. Financial problems meant they had to resign from Wearside League in 1982 and join the Tyneside Amateur League as Heaton United in 1982/83 season. Won this league the following season back as Heaton Stannington, then spent 2 seasons in the Northern Amateur League and 27 seasons in Northern Alliance. Returned to Northern League Division 2 for 2013/14 season.

After postponements due to a frozen pitch on the previous two Wednesday nights, this match finally took place at the third time of asking. Grounsell Park is the closest Northern League ground to my house, so after a brisk walk I met Robbo outside of the ground and we took an elevated position on the terrace next to the clubhouse, giving us a good view of the action.

Morpeth are flying high in the Northern Premier League East Division (Step 4 of the non-league pyramid, two leagues above The Stan) and they had a good travelling support for this Northumberland Senior Cup Quarter Final tie. It did not take long before they were celebrating taking the lead – Jack Foalle rounding Stan keeper Daniel Regan on 11 minutes, after a spell of almost constant pressure from the visitors from the kick-off. For the first half hour, Morpeth continued to show their superior pace and skill but they could not add to their one goal lead against the tenacious home team. On 31 minutes, against the run of play, Stan equalised when Joe Kerridge slid the ball past Morpeth keeper Dimitris Tsapalos after their best move of the half so far. It remained all square at half time and we went for a pint of real ale in the clubhouse (that proudly declares it was voted CAMRA's best club in Tyneside in 2018) reflecting on what had been an exciting first half, albeit most of it taking place in Stan's half of the pitch. The local stand-up comedian Gavin Webster, who is a big Stan fan, was sitting on the table next to us. I pointed him out to Robbo who seemed to get him mixed up with Kevin Webster – i.e. a fictional character from Coronation Street!

Morpeth started the second half where they left off in the first, pinning Stan back. They regained the lead after 55 minutes via a long range shot from Stuart Mott (a goal that we missed due to still being in the clubhouse finishing off our drinks). We went back outside and stood behind The Stan goalmouth where we reckoned most of the second half action would take place, and we were not wrong. Morpeth kept up the constant pressure on The Stan goal trying to kill the game off but they were denied 3 times in 3 minutes around the hour mark by 3 good saves from Regan. It was proving to be a cracking cup tie with non-stop action. The visitors' dominance eventually paid off on 84 minutes – Julian Petrache heading the ball into the top of the net from a corner to make it 3-1. We had a great view of that goal. A late Stan penalty converted into the top corner by Connor Campbell proved to be merely a consolation goal. Overall, Morpeth's extra pace and class showed and they deserved their win, but Stan put in a good battling performance to make it a thoroughly enjoyable cup-tie. I walked the 2 miles back home making the 4 mile round walking trip to Grounsell Park a good stretch of the legs on a chilly Wednesday night.

Vital Statistics:

Heaton Stannington 2 (Kerridge 31, Campbell 90 pen)
Morpeth Town 3 (Foalle 11, Mott 55, Petrache 83)
Northumberland Senior Cup Quarter Final
Admission - £5
Programme – £1
Attendance – 240

STOCKTON WIN IN WINDY WHITLEY
Northern League Ground 17

Saturday 9th February 2019
WHITLEY BAY
Hillheads Park, Rink Way, off Hillheads Way, Whitley Bay, Tyne and Wear

Formed in 1950 as Whitley Bay Athletic and played in Northern Alliance. Joined the North Eastern League in 1955. In 1958 they dropped Athletic from the club name and joined the Northern League. Joined the Northern Premier League in 1987/88 season. Won Division 1 championship and promotion to Premier Division in 1990/91.Highest ever finish in 1993/94 season (11th). Relegated back to Northern League in 2000.

FA Vase winners (2001/02, 2008/09, 2010/11 and 2011/12 - first team to win it 4 times).

Northern League champions (1964/65, 1965/66, 2006/07)

Northern League Cup winners (1964/65, 1970/71)

Northumberland Senior Cup winners 12 times, most recently in 2010.

Best performance in FA Cup - 3rd Round in 1989/90.

I met Mark (second appearance after his debut at North Shields in October 2018) at 1 pm and we took the Metro from South Gosforth to Whitley Bay. I had not seen him for two months. He had been away in Australia and Dubai for most of December with his wife, where they had red hot temperatures that were at the exact opposite end of the temperature scale that I experienced on my visit to Consett in December. We called into the Phoenix Tap pub, that is close to the ground on Hillheads Road, for a couple of pre-match pints and a catch up – and very pleasant it was too. When the barman changed the TV to the live Scotland v Ireland Six Nations Rugby match, it signalled it was time to drink up and leave – Mark not being a fan of the giant egg chasers. We took the short five-minute walk to the ground, and sat in the main stand to try to get a bit of shelter from the wind (that weather forecasters were calling Storm Erik).

The referee was a woman – Helen Conley from Bishop Auckland. All the previous Northern League matches I had attended had been refereed by a man and I did not realise that there was a female referee on the Northern League circuit. (Kev Larkham later told me that she has been the woman in black for a number of years and also runs the line at higher levels). Male or female, the referee is of course equally likely to receive some abuse from fans for decisions they do not agree with. Sometimes it is good natured banter and sometimes it is more vitriolic. It was disappointing though that one of Helen's decisions against Whitley after about half an hour was greeted with a shout of "Get back into the kitchen" from a man behind us in the stand. Like many others, I find this sort of comment offensive and tiresome. Sadly, I feel sure she has heard that comment before though – and probably much worse.

Both sides were finding it hard to play any decent football in the strong wind. A poor first half ended without a single shot on target from either team. Shortly after the break, the visitors took the lead when Joe Taylor's corner on 52 minutes was headed into the net by Michael Roberts on the 6 yard box. The second period was slightly less windy and much more entertaining. On 71 minutes, Roberts got his and Stockton's second goal after a good team passing move. It felt like Stockton had done enough to secure the 3 points, but Whitley had a late surge and missed a couple of really good chances. Overall, the visitors' solid second half performance in the testing conditions gave them what we thought was a deserved win – their fifth league win in a row.

Vital Statistics:

Whitley Bay 0 Stockton Town 2 (Roberts 52, 71)
Northern League Division 1
Admission - £6
Programme – £1.50
Attendance – 271
........MISSION......COMPLETION IN SIGHT......

KNOCKING ON HEBBURN'S DOOR
Northern League Ground 18

Saturday 16th February 2019
HEBBURN TOWN
The Energy Check Sports Ground, South Drive, Hebburn, Tyne and Wear

Formed in 1912 as works team for the Reyrolles company. Played in Jarrow and District Junior League, South Shields Combination League (from 1918), Tyneside Combination (from 1923), Tyneside League (from 1927), Northern Combination (from 1941), North Eastern League (from 1959) and Wearside League (from 1960).

Promoted to Northern League Division 2 in 1989 and promoted to Division 1 at end of 1991/92 season. Relegated back to Division 2 in 1994/95 due to ground issues. Promoted 1999/2000, relegated 2000/01, promoted 2011/12, relegated 2013/14 and promoted 2017/18 as Division 2 Runners-up.

Durham Challenge Cup winners (1942/43 and 1991/92),

Best performance in FA Cup – 4th Qualifying Round (2011/12).

I had not intended to go to a match today due to going to a concert at Sage Gateshead in the evening (for the record, to see Simply Dylan – a Bob Dylan tribute band). By mid-morning however, given that it was a dry and bright day with only a slight wind, I decided that it was too good a day to not go to a match. I opted for the relatively short journey to Hebburn (a 25 minute Metro journey from home) for their match against West Auckland, knowing that I could be back home after the match in good time to go out again for the concert.

I arrived at Hebburn Metro station at 2.30 pm and it was a ten minute walk from there to the ground. On the way I noticed that all cyclists, whether adults or children, rode their bikes on the pavement – I am not sure if this is unique to Hebburn but I have not noticed it anywhere else. I also passed the Hebburn Protestant Conservative Club - a social club that I would struggle to be accepted as a member of, on both religious and political grounds.

The Energy Check Sports Ground is a pretty impressive set up. Exterior and interior refurbishment in 2017/18 has produced a modern clubhouse with quality outdoor decking with tables and seating, and a large stand.

The teams had met here a week earlier in the Last 16 of the FA Vase – West Auckland winning 2-0 in front of a crowd of 1,310. There was a considerably lower crowd here today, but with Hebburn lying 7th in the league and West in 8th place, I was hoping it would be an exciting close encounter – and it certainly was. West took the lead after 18 minutes, when Amar Purewal neatly despatched a penalty, sending Hebburn keeper Andrew Jennison the wrong way. On the half hour the home side equalised – Louis Storey slotting the ball past West's keeper Shane Bland. The sides went into the break level.

The second half kicked off at a higher tempo and the visitors regained their lead after 51 minutes - David Dowson firing a left footed shot into the top corner from a Liam Hegarty throw in. Just after the hour mark, Hegarty received a red card for a high challenge on Hebburn's Andrew Stephenson, although the West dugout thought otherwise and let the referee know in no uncertain terms. Hebburn levelled again on 76 minutes with an emphatic penalty from Luke Sullivan. The third penalty of the match was awarded to West on 79 minutes. Purewal stepped up again but his spot kick rattled off the cross bar and was headed away to safety by Luke Gilhespy. A very exciting period of stoppage time saw West take the lead on 94 minutes for the third time via the fourth penalty award of the match - Adam Mitchell firing the ball low beyond Jennison. Two minutes later, with almost the final kick of the game, Hebburn's Graeme Armstrong steered Michael Richardson's cross past Bland, to equalise for the third time and give them a share of the spoils.

I caught the Metro back home feeling very pleased I had made the effort to witness a cracking game of football between two well matched teams. After refuelling, I headed back out with my mate Ron for an evening of Bob Dylan songs (the man who wrote 'Knocking On Heaven's Door').

Vital Statistics:

Hebburn Town 3 (Storey 29, Sullivan 76 pen, Armstrong 96)

West Auckland Town 3 (Purewal 18 pen, Dowson 51, Mitchell 94 pen)

Northern League Division 1

Admission - £6

Programme – £2

Attendance – 210

BONNY BLUES' REVENGE
Northern League Ground 19

Saturday 23rd February 2019
PENRITH
The Frenchfield Stadium, Carleton, Penrith, Cumbria

Formed in 1894. Played in the North Eastern League and Carlisle and District League. Joined the Northern League in 1948. Moved to North West Counties League in 1982 and joined the Northern Premier League in 1987. Relegated back to North West Counties League in 1990 then returned to the Northern League in 1997. Changed name to Penrith Town in 2007 but a merger with Penrith United in 2008 saw them revert back to Penrith name. Nicknamed The Bonny Blues

Northern League Division 1 runners-up (1961/62)

Northern League Division 2 champions (2002/03 and 2007/08)

Won Cumberland Cup 16 times (most recently in 2010)

Best performance in FA Cup – 2nd Round Proper (1981/82)

Anita and I had planned this trip to Penrith (one of the longest journeys on The Mission at around 75 miles from home) at the beginning of the year, knowing there was always a good chance we would need to postpone it to attend a match in March or April instead, given the poor weather Penrith due to its location can so often experience in February. However, it turned out to be a glorious day for the time of year– sunshine, no rain forecast, not too cold and just a little bit windy. We arrived at the Frenchfield Stadium just after 2 pm. It is in a lovely rural setting, surrounded by tree lined low hills. It has a modern clubhouse but still maintains a traditional old style feel.

We sat in the stand, three rows from the front right on the halfway line with a great view of the action. A good contingent of visiting Stockton fans had made the journey from Teesside to Cumbria. Their team was on a good run of form, lying 5th in the Northern League Division 1 after 6 games unbeaten, and 10 days earlier they had beaten Consett to reach the semi-final of the League Cup. In the reverse of this fixture last October, they had thrashed Penrith 8-0. The Bonny Blues were lying rock bottom of the division, 12 points behind 2nd bottom Whickham, but they had shown some signs of improvement lately.

On a bobbly pitch, there was a scrappy start to the match with Penrith not allowing the visitors the chance to play their passing game, winning most of the 50-50 balls and creating some opportunities for their strikers by pumping long balls up front missing out the midfield area. Penrith had a few chances in the first half hour but Stockton managed to defend their goal. On 40 minutes though, it was the visitors who took an unlikely lead - Max Craggs superbly curling a free kick from 20 yards into the top right hand corner of the net, giving Blues keeper Stuart Dixon no chance. Straight from the restart, Penrith equalised – Martyn Coleman heading home from an Angelos Leftheriadis' cross – to send the teams in level at half time.

The home side were quickest out of the blocks in the second half and immediately put the Stockton defence under pressure again. They almost scored on 46 minutes when a shot from Coleman was parried onto the bar by Stockton keeper Josh Moody. They did take a deserved lead on 52 minutes – Max Brown slotting home a long ball delivery from Leftheriadis. The visitors made some substitutions and around the hour mark they started to have their best spell of the match. They came close to equalising when Dixon tipped Nathan Mulligan's header onto the bar, and again when Penrith defender Matty Clarke deflected Craggs' shot over the bar from a few yards out. On 83 minutes, Blues substitute Shaun Gardner scored with his first touch to settle the contest. A jubilant Penrith fan standing at the side of the pitch in front of the stand celebrated the third goal by hugging the nearest person to him - who turned out to be a Stockton fan. He could be excused given that they had not had much to shout about this season so far.

We felt privileged to have witnessed Penrith's first home league win of the season. They totally upset the form book and out fought Stockton today, thoroughly deserving their victory.

Vital Statistics:

Penrith 3 (Coleman 41, Brown 52, Gardner 83)

Stockton Town 1 (Craggs 40)

Northern League Division 1

Admission - £6

Programme – £1

Attendance – 148

PLANE SPOTTING
Northern League Ground 20

Wednesday 27th February 2019
WEST ALLOTMENT CELTIC
Druid Park, Callerton Lane, Woolsington, Newcastle upon Tyne

Formed in 1928 in West Allotment village in North Tyneside. Played for 55 years in junior leagues. Joined Northern Alliance in 1983 – won the title 8 times.

Joined Northern League Division 2 in 2004, champions in 2004/05 and promoted to Division 1. Relegated to Division 2 in 2011.

Have played at grounds in North Tyneside at Holystone, West Allotment (Farm Ground), Backworth, Whitley Bay and Benton. Moved out of North Tyneside to Druid Park for 2017/18 season.

After a short trip on the Metro, I met Mark at Callerton Parkway Metro Station at 7 pm. From here it was quite literally a 2 minute walk to West Allotment's current ground. We had a pre-match pint in the very well-appointed clubhouse (that was among the best I had been to so far on my Northern League travels). We soon discovered that an evening match at Druid Park is a fairly unique experience. The ground is very close to Newcastle Airport. It has a 4G pitch, no seated area or terracing, and even with its good floodlights, the ground has an isolated dark feel to it. Planes flying fairly low over the pitch as they take off from the nearby runways of the airport only add to its uniqueness.

At the kick off, we stood at the side of the pitch opposite the dugouts amongst some of the good number of North Shields fans that had travelled here for this Northumberland Senior Cup Semi Final tie. With the glittering prize of playing in the Final at Newcastle United's St James Park stadium at stake, a keen contest was anticipated.

The teams are a division apart (Shields are 4th in Division 1 and Allotment are 10th in Division 2) but it was the home team that had the better early chances to score in the first quarter of an hour. After 20 minutes, play went back and forth with a couple of chances for both sides but good defending kept it goalless. The deadlock was broken on 30 minutes when Shields' striker Gary Day scored from close range after some good work by Jordan Summerly. On 33 minutes a header from Ryan Carr just missed the target for the visitors, and on 35 minutes Michael Baxter sliced a shot wide for Allotment. It remained 0-1 at the break after a pretty even first half. We had a half time Bovril in the clubhouse as the night had become a lot colder.

The second half kicked off and it was clear that Allotment were still very much in the tie. It felt like Shields needed to score again to make it safe. The visitors created a few good efforts at goal but Allotment defended well. With around 15 minutes left it was Allotment who suddenly created a few chances, the best of them on 85 minutes when Shields' full back Jack Donnison cleared the ball off the goal line after a scramble in the penalty area. There was a frantic last few minutes with the home side desperately trying to find the equaliser but Shields held out to reach the Final. I felt they just about deserved it on the night, but Allotment gave it their all and it did not feel like the teams were a division apart tonight.

Mark and I retreated to the comfort of the clubhouse for a couple of post-match pints and a discussion on a variety of topics – from football to Brexit and everything in between. And for the record, we spotted 5 planes taking off in total tonight.

Vital Statistics:

West Allotment Celtic 0 North Shields 1 (Day 30)

Northumberland Senior Cup Semi Final

Admission - £6

Programme – £1

Attendance – 270

Saturday 9th March 2019
Gateshead versus Barnet
Gateshead International Stadium

I had not been to a Gateshead match for over two months. There had been a great deal of turmoil at the club during this time, with the off the field situation looking very precarious. On 10th January, manager Steve Watson and assistant Mickey Cummins resigned and accepted an offer to manage National League North side York City. On 1st February, long term General Manager Mike Coulson resigned (he later joined Blyth Spartans in a similar role). Two key players (Scott Boden and Fraser Kerr) were sold in February, reputedly to pay tax owed to HMRC. This reduced the senior squad to 16. The club is currently subject to a transfer embargo due to exceeding the budget they set and agreed with the National League at the start of the season. Chairman/owner (Ranjan Varghese) and Chief Financial Advisor (Joe Cala) have continually evaded adequately answering fans' concerns about the current and future financial stability of the club. Only days before today's match they dodged another bullet when a Winding Up Order due to non-payment of another £20,000 tax bill was dismissed (debt still to be paid ASAP though). Then, the day before the match, the owner announced that the club was to be put up for sale, prompting the supporters' group to cancel a planned peaceful protest that was due to take place immediately after today's game.

In complete contrast to these worrying events, the young team on the field were currently sitting in the promotion play-off places and had gone on an excellent unbeaten run of 7 league games since Watson left and Ben Clark (ex-captain and stalwart central defender) moved up from reserve team coach to be first team manager.

As detailed in Chapters 2 and 3, Gateshead Football Club has a long history of ups and downs and highs and lows but today it felt that this current situation was a new record low. All the players could do of course was to continue to produce great performances and all the fans could do was to continue to support them. As one of these fans for 50 years and counting, I drove over to the GIS in good time for the kick off and met up with Ken at our usual seats. I had not seen him since the Hartlepool match on Boxing Day so as we watched the match we had a good catch up chat, which was predominately about the situation at the club of course.

The opening period of the game was pretty even. Heed striker Steve Rigg headed just wide on 8 minutes from a lovely Connor Thomson cross. Minutes later Barnet went close to scoring, when Dan Sweeney's goal bound header from a Medy Elito corner was headed over the bar by The Heed's Robbie Tinkler. Elito had certainly been a handful on the left wing up to this point. The visitors did take the lead on 24 minutes when Ephron Mason-Clark just beat the offside trap and slipped the ball past keeper Aynsley Pears. Four minutes later Gateshead should have equalised, when Rigg had a one on one with Barnet keeper Mark Cousins, but his shot bounced back off the post and, with an open goal, he put the rebound wide. In first half stoppage time, Barnet's Shaquille Coulthirst was sent off after receiving his second yellow card for some persistent Oscar winning play acting.

Ben Clark's half time team talk must have been inspirational, as The Heed came out firing on all cylinders. Within 3 minutes they were level – Mike Williamson passed to Thomson out wide, who crossed for Greg Olley to slide the ball home. Gateshead were in the ascendency after this with the extra man advantage, and they took the lead on 72 minutes when Tom White curled a shot just inside the post. As is generally the norm with The Heed the last ten minutes proved a bit nervy as the visitors dropped their defensive tactics and pressed for an equaliser. The Heed held out for another vital 3 points to stay in the play-off places.

Promotion to EFL League Two via the play-offs, or (given all the off the field shenanigans) playing in a much lower league than the National League next season, or even not playing at all – at the final whistle today it was still anyone's guess.

Vital Statistics:

Gateshead 2 (Olley 48, White 72) Barnet 1 (Mason-Clark 24)
National League
Admission - £15
Programme – didn't buy one
Attendance – 665 (115 away fans)

STOCKTON SUCCESS
Northern League Ground 21

Wednesday 20th March 2019
STOCKTON TOWN
Coverall Stadium, Bishopton Road West, Stockton on Tees

Formed in 1979 as Hartburn Juniors. Changed name to Stockton Town in 2003. Joined Teesside League 2nd Division in 2009/10 and Wearside League in 2010/11. Wearside League champions 4 seasons in a row (from 2012/13 to 2015/16), also did the double winning Wearside League Cup in 2015/16, and a clean sweep quadruple in 2014/15 winning the Wearside League Cup, the Monkwearmouth Cup and Shipowners Cup. Nicknamed The Anchors

Promoted to Northern League Division 2 in 2016, won title and promotion to Division 1 in first season.

FA Vase runners up in 2017/18.

After watching Stockton Town playing away from home three times this season, I visited their home ground tonight for their game against Newcastle Benfield to complete the current 18 Northern League Division 1 grounds. I was joined by Kev, and this seemed appropriate given that we had attended the first game of my Mission together at Sunderland RCA in August last year. It was also Kev's 38th Benfield match this season – some achievement!

We parked in the carpark of the Sixth Form College adjoining the ground and had a pre-match drink in the modern, heavily Stockton Town FC branded sports bar / clubhouse, that was located in another building quite separate from the 3G pitch. It is a slightly unusual set up but clearly one that works to the mutual benefit of club and college – the 3G pitch is used by the college students during the week and also available for hire by groups for 7 a side matches. At the kick-off we stood behind the dugouts with what appeared to be possibly the only other 2 Benfield fans who had travelled down to Teesside for tonight's match – one was on video camera duty and one was on Twitter updates duty. When Benfield went behind early on to a Michael Roberts goal following some mazy dribbling from winger Kev Hayes, we moved away to another part of the ground to save the video cameraman the job of having to edit out any possible bad language from his video footage later on. Both teams were playing some nice passing football at a good pace, but Benfield did not have any cutting edge in the final third, whereas Stockton created a few chances. On 28 minutes Stockton's Nathan Mulligan suffered a nasty injury (suspected broken collarbone) following a collision with one of his teammates when both going for the same ball. Minutes later Stockton went 2-0 up, Michael Roberts grabbing his second goal with a header from a Max Craggs' cross. The first half ended with the visitors not having had a meaningful shot on target.

Benfield started with more purpose after the interval but still could not trouble the Stockton goal, which we were standing behind for the second half. With 20 minutes left, Benfield's Reece Noble fouled Stockton's James Risbrough on the halfway line and the ref deemed it to be a red card rather than a yellow. Kev shouted loudly in disagreement, calling the referee a few names ('a clown' being the mildest of them) but he escaped a red card. Almost immediately after play restarted, the 10 men went 3-0 down when Fred Woodhouse scored after some good build up play from Hayes and Peter Bulmer. In the final throes of the match, Benfield manager Stuart Elliott called the ref 'clueless' resulting in him being sent from the dugouts. The game was totally put to bed on 86 minutes when Hayes added a 4th goal for the hosts, smashing a left foot shot into the bottom left hand corner from 18 yards out.

As we drove back north on the A19, Kev was delighted that I had achieved my aim of visiting all 18 Northern League Division 1 grounds during the season. He was less delighted about Benfield losing their last 2 league games and leaking 4 goals in each. I had now watched Benfield 6 times this season with Kev and it certainly had been a mixed bag of good, bad and ugly.

Vital Statistics:

Stockton Town 4 (Roberts 6, 30, Woodhouse 73, Hayes 86) Newcastle Benfield 0

Northern League Division 1

Admission - £7

Programme – £1

Attendance – 315

……MISSION…..ACCOMPLISHED…….

Tuesday 26th March 2019
Dunston UTS versus Guisborough Town
The UTS Stadium, Wellington Road, Dunston

With a 12 point lead at the top of the Northern League Division 1, Dunston only needed 1 more point from their remaining 6 matches to be crowned champions. After visiting all the grounds in the league during the season, and given that The UTS Stadium is only a short car journey from home, it seemed appropriate to attend the match where they could possibly clinch the title. It did not seem so appropriate for any of my other usual travelling companions though, so I went to it on my own.

There was a decent sized crowd who like me were expecting Dunston to be totally pumped up to win tonight. I stood in the covered area behind the dugouts. The champions elect made the perfect start, taking the lead after only 4 minutes. It was a spectacular goal (a video of it was later shown to the wider British public on Sky Sports News). Guisborough keeper Jordan Nixon fired a free kick from just inside his own half (never a good idea to have goalkeepers taking free kicks there in my opinion) into the Dunston penalty area, where Dunston's Liam Brooks hit an 85 yard long range effort on goal, that bounced twice and hit the bar as Nixon ran back to his goalmouth. From the rebound off the bar, an unmarked Mark Fitzpartrick headed the ball home from inside the six-yard box. There was an initial sense of job done from the crowd but Guisborough, who are still in a relegation battle, gradually settled into the match and they equalised on 14 minutes through Daniel Earl's left footed shot into the bottom corner. I moved out of the covered area and stood a bit further down on the same side of the pitch. Here I bumped into Tenerife Dave (so nicknamed due to his love of holidays on that sunny island). Like me, he is a long standing and long-suffering Gateshead FC fan. We had some good craic whilst watching the rest of the game. The remainder of the first half was pretty even with a couple of reasonable chances for both sides, but they went in level at half time.

The second half started at the same fast tempo. Brooks hit the bar for Dunston and Luke Nixon shot just over the bar for Guisborough. On the hour mark, Fitzpatrick had the ball in the visitors' net but it was ruled offside. Minutes later Dunston went back in front when Jack Elliott, following a pacey run down the left wing, smashed the ball past keeper Nixon into the roof of the net. Guisborough never gave up but Dunston's win and the Division 1 title was secured on 75 minutes – Fitzpatrick slotting the ball home after receiving a defence splitting pass from Scott Heslop. At the final whistle there were rightful ecstatic celebrations from the players, coaching staff and fans. I have watched Dunston 3 times this season and they have been very impressive each time. They seem well equipped to do well in their move up to Step 4 non-league level next season.

Vital Statistics:

Dunston UTS 3 (Fitzpatrick 4, 75, Elliott 65)

Guisborough Town 1 (Earl 14)

Northern League Division 1

Admission - £6

Programme – £1

Attendance – 437

Saturday 6th April 2019
Newcastle United versus Crystal Palace
St James' Park, Newcastle upon Tyne

When my friend Alan contacted me to say there was a spare ticket for this match, I was initially in two minds. I had of course not been to a Toon match for a number of years for reasons outlined in a Chapter 3 of this book. I decided though, that after spending the whole of this season so far attending non-league matches, it was time to return to St James' Park for a very different kind of experience.

I walked from home across the vast open space of Newcastle Town Moor. At one point a group of 4 cows that were approaching the main path in a row from the left, stopped to let me pass then carried on crossing the main path. Very polite of them I thought. On reaching the Haymarket area of the city centre at around 2.15 all the pubs were full of Newcastle fans having pre-match refreshments. The streets were packed with people – anyone who was not going to the match would likely be spending the afternoon in the shops – I know what I prefer. I met Alan at 2.30 and we climbed up a few flights of stairs to our seats near the back of the top tier of the Gallowgate End. I commented to Alan that having spent the season watching matches from the touchline and seeing the whites of the players' eyes, it was disappointing to be watching from 100 yards away and hardly being able to make out the numbers on the players' shirts. He grunted something about how I had turned into a typical non-league fan now.

Although it had been 9 years since I regularly attended games at St James Park (my seat in the Milburn Stand when I had a season ticket was a damn sight closer than the one I had for this match) some things had not changed. The ubiquitous adverts for owner Mike Ashley's Sport Direct business for example – and the fact that Newcastle lost the match. Overall, Newcastle had the most possession and the most shots. However, they were guilty of not taking the chances created with some poor finishing and poor final balls. Striker Salomon Rondon had the ball in the net after 15 minutes but was correctly judged to have been marginally offside. Palace's James Tomkins shot past Martin Dubravka into the net a few minutes before half time, but this was also correctly disallowed as James McArthur was judged to have impeded The Toon keeper, standing in front of him in an offside position. For all of Newcastle's domination it was Palace's Wilfred Zaha that looked to be the best player on the pitch. He caused the home team's defence some anxious moments with his skill and trickery. With 10 minutes of normal time remaining (there was to be 7 minutes of additional time due to a second half knee injury requiring a stretcher to Newcastle defender Florian Lejeune) Zaha was tripped in the box by DeAndre Yedlin (who had a woeful match). Luka Milivojevic blasted the penalty kick home (he has scored 10 out of 11 penalties in the league this season). Palace held on to claim the win that put them onto 39 points and relative safety. The defeat left Newcastle on 35 points and likely still needing another win from their last 5 games to avoid relegation.

After the match I walked back home over the Town Moor. It was cold and grey with a light drizzly rain, which was a perfect backdrop for the mood of The Toon fans.

Vital Statistics:

Newcastle United 0 Crystal Palace 1 (Milivojevic pen 81)
Premier League
Admission - £25
Programme – didn't buy one
Attendance – 51,926

The final Northern League Division 1 matches of the season took place last Saturday and today the curtain was brought down on the Division 2 season. Billingham Town only needed a draw in their final match to clinch the league title, but a defeat coupled with Thornaby beating Esh Winning would hand the title to their Teesside rivals. Thornaby had been on an incredible run, winning their last 14 league games (including a 2-1 home win over Billingham in early March) but Billingham still had their destiny in their own hands. Stan were guaranteed a respectable 4th place finish irrespective of today's result.

It was a gloriously sunny day as I joined Kev and Robbo at Grounsell Park. We stood on the grass bank near the dugouts amongst the large contingent of away fans that had travelled here to hopefully see their team finish the job. The opening period showed that Stan were not just going to give them an easy ride though. Town took the lead after 15 minutes when Stan keeper Dan Regan fumbled the ball into his own net from a corner. Seven minutes later, Connor Campbell equalised for Stan, neatly slipping the ball past the advancing Town keeper Lewis McDonald. The visitors restored their lead on 36 minutes when Craig Hutchinson buried the ball into the bottom corner. This was his 43rd goal in Division 2 this season – an amazing tally at any level of football - and he is far and away the league's top scorer. It remained 2-1 at half time, but with Thornaby also winning, Billingham still had work to do in the second half to be confirmed as league champions.

In the second half, given that a draw would suffice, Billingham looked content to defend their lead. Stan played some good football but could not find a way past Town's well organised and resolute defence. The visitors were always dangerous on the break as Stan pressed forward, and Hutchinson should have put the game to bed on 80 minutes but he missed a great chance from 6 yards. There was a serious injury to Stan's Joseph Fulcher on 84 minutes, and Kev quipped that he looked likely to be out for the rest of the season.

Billingham saw the game out to win 2-1. At the final whistle, their euphoric fans ran onto the pitch to celebrate with the players. We watched the presentation of the trophy, signalling that the Northern League 2018/19 season was now over. My own Northern League journey this season had started on the opening day in August with Kev on a sunny afternoon in Ryhope and had ended on an equally sunny afternoon with him in Heaton – perfect bookends.

Vital Statistics:

Heaton Stannington 1 (Campbell 22)
Billingham Town 2 (Regan og 15, Hutchinson 36)
Northern League Division 2
Admission - £5
Programme – £1
Attendance – 401

Saturday 27th April 2019
Gateshead versus Barrow
Gateshead International Stadium

This was the last match of the season for The Heed. Whether it was to be the last match they ever played at the GIS or the last match ever that this squad of players played together remained to be seen. Since my last visit to the ground in March, the off the field situation at the club had become even more precarious. There had been organised fans' protests against the current owners before and after matches, the ongoing it's on / it's off sale of the club situation and talk of forming a phoenix club. The only certainty at Gateshead FC today was uncertainty.

I had been in two minds about going to this game. There was nothing to play for, The Heed having just missed out on a play off place after losing away to Harrogate on Easter Monday. My brother Kev was visiting from Liverpool for the weekend and he convinced me to go on the basis that it could be a significant game in the club's history, or even unthinkably, the end of the club's history. We had been to see the band Half Man Half Biscuit at The Boiler Shop in Newcastle the night before. One of the songs they performed 'The Light at the End of the Tunnel is the Light of an Oncoming Train' sadly seemed appropriate for today.

Barrow made a flying start to the match and were a goal up after only 8 minutes via a curling shot from John Rooney (Wayne's brother) that beat Heed keeper Aynsley Pears and nestled just inside the post. The visitors were well in control and midway through the first half Rooney scored another almost identical goal. The Heed woke up towards the end of the first half but Barrow defended comfortably and went into the interval 2-0 up. Gateshead improved considerably in the second half but barely troubled the Barrow goal. Ten minutes from the end The Heed's Tom White was sent off for a second bookable offence (dissent).

After the final whistle, Kev was impressed that a Heed fan behind us congratulated two Barrow fans on a deserved win, representing what he feels should be the true spirit of football. I agree with him of course. The Gateshead players huddled in the centre of the pitch with manager Ben Clark and the coaching staff for a few minutes, and then they walked off to salute The Heed fans. Whether this was to be the final salute in a Gateshead shirt from many of these players is not certain, but there can be no denying that they have performed exceptionally well this season, with an eventual 9th place league position. My brother was right– it did feel like a significant day in Gateshead FC's history and I was pleased that we had attended today. However, we were feeling a bit deflated that our hometown team that we regularly supported together during the 1970s/early 1980s before Kev relocated to Liverpool, was in such a perilous state. As a famous Liverpool band once sang, we still 'walk on with hope in our hearts' though.

Vital Statistics:

Gateshead 0 Barrow 2 (Rooney 8, 22)

National League

Admission - £15

Programme – didn't buy one

Attendance – 798 (180 away fans)

Post script - Gateshead had had an exceptional season on the pitch but were in complete turmoil off the pitch. At the end of May 2019 a new consortium headed up by a businessman who had been a lifelong Heed fan bought the club. Disappointingly, on 8th June 2019 the National League confirmed that, due to the Varghese/Cala regime's mismanagement during this season, Gateshead were relegated to play in the National League North in the 2019/20 season. However, the change of ownership certainly signalled better times ahead.

CHAPTER

DIVISION 2 WITH THE HAPPY FEW

AROUND THE NORTHERN LEAGUE GROUNDS

(Part 3 – August to November 2019)

I thoroughly enjoyed completing The Mission and now felt like a proper groundhopper. For the 2019/20 season, my aims were to visit the grounds of the three Northern League Division 1 teams that were promoted from last season's Division 2 to recomplete Division 1, and visit the fifteen remaining Division 2 grounds I had not already been to.

As you would probably expect, the average attendances in Division 2 are lower than Division 1. A few clubs regularly have crowds in double figures not triple figures but the loyalty of the supporters and club volunteers certainly matches that of Division 1. I stole a line from Shakespeare's 'Henry V' describing them as 'The Happy Few' and I called this new season's groundhopping venture, with no prizes for creativity, The Second Mission.

Feeling like a frustrated wannabe football journalist who had missed his vocation earlier in life, I started writing reports on this season's games and posting them on my newly created blog;

The Casual Bystander - https://wordpress.com/home/stout-hearted.blog.

Double figures rather than triple figures would also be the truest way to describe the readership of my blog, but I have been pleased to receive some good feedback not just from friends but also on social media from supporters and officials from some of the Division 2 clubs I have written about.

…….SECOND MISSION…..GREEN FOR GO……

PLAYING AWAY AT HOME...
Northern League Ground 22

Saturday 3rd August 2019
DURHAM CITY / WILLINGTON
Hall Lane, Willington, County Durham

Durham City: Established in 1918 and competed for one season in the Victory League formed in celebration of the end of the First World War. They played in the Football League (Third Division North) from 1921 to 1928. Folded in 1938, re-established in 1949. Joined Northern League in 1952. Won first Northern League Division 1 title in 1993/94, relegated to Division 2 in 1997/98, promoted back to Division 1 in 1998/99. Promoted to Northern Premier League (Division 1 North) in 2007/08 but lost main sponsor and following exodus of players returned to Northern League Division 1 at end of 2011/12 season. Relegated to Division 2 in 2015/16. Northern Premier League Division 1 North champions 2008/09. Northern League Cup winners 2001/02. Durham Challenge Cup winners 1971/72

Best performance in FA Cup – 2nd Round in 1925/26, 1957/58

Best performance in FA Vase – Semi Final 2001/02

Willington: Established in 1906. Joined Northern League in 1911, champions for the first of 3 times in 1913/14. FA Amateur Cup finalists in 1938/39 and winners in 1949/50 (beat Bishop Auckland 4-0 at Wembley, attendance 88,000). Relegated from Northern League Division 1 to Division 2 in 1982/83. Only finished in Top Ten 5 times in 22 seasons. Relegated to Wearside League in 2005/06. Promoted back to Northern League Division 2 in 2012/13. Northern League champions 1913/14, 1925/26, 1929/30. Northern League Cup winners 1924/25, 1925/26, 1927/28, 1930/31, 1931/32, 1948/49, 1956/57 and 1974/75

..... That is what Willington AFC (affectionately known as Willo) found themselves doing on the opening day of the 2019/20 Northern League Division 2 season. Their opponents Durham City are playing their home games this season at Willo's Hall Lane ground, so when the Northern League's computer (if there is such a thing) generated Durham City v Willington as the season opener, Willo found themselves occupying the away dressing room and dugout on their home patch.

Just before kick-off, I got chatting at the Tea Bar to the lady who washes the Willo players' strips (this week that would mean washing their striking pink shirts – their away strip of course). She told me that 9 players from last season's squad had left to join local Division 2 rivals Tow Law Town. This seems particularly extreme to me.

Two weeks ago manager Stephen Skinner left and Ibby Hassan took over with full back Craig Ruddy as his player/assistant manager. This all meant that Willo took to the field with a new look playing squad and management team. Despite all this upheaval they, perhaps unsurprisingly, looked more at home than Durham City today. Striker Ashley Davis saw a scorching shot rattle the bar after 20 minutes and they opened the scoring on 35 minutes through Callum Forster's cool finish. Debutant Liam Lawlor headed home from a corner on 57 minutes to give Willo a deserved 2-0 lead. Durham pressed to get back into the match but their finishing was poor. I can only recall them seriously testing Willo keeper Kieron Proctor once. Overall, I felt the away team deserved their win.

Vital Statistics:

Durham City 0 Willington 2 (Forster 35, Lawlor 57)

Northern League Division 2

Admission £5

Programme £1

Attendance 96

…..SECOND MISSION…..COMMENCED……

UNIVERSITY EDUCATION FOR STAN
Northern League Ground 23

Monday 5th August 2019
NEWCASTLE UNIVERSITY
Kimberley Park, Prudhoe, Northumberland

Established in the 1970s and played in the Northern Alliance. Won the Premier Division of the Northern Alliance in 2017/18 season. Promoted to Northern League Division 2 at the end of the 2018/19 season. Known as The Royals.

On a sunny Monday evening, Robbo and I headed out west from Newcastle to the Northumbrian outpost of Prudhoe. Specifically, we travelled to Kimberley Park, where Division 2 new boys Newcastle University (The Uni) will play their home matches in their first season at this level. Their opponents tonight were Robbo and I's local non-league team Heaton Stannington (The Stan) with both teams looking for their first points after losing their season openers two days ago. The 7.30 pm kick off meant the floodlights were not needed until midway through the second half. I love watching football in these t-shirt wearing conditions and making the most of it, being only too aware that I will soon be freezing to the bone watching midweek evening kick off matches in the autumn/winter months.

The Stan got off to a flying start with 2 goals in the first 5 minutes. With 3 minutes gone, Regan Paterson dribbled around Uni keeper Shaun Blackhouse and slotted the ball in. Two minutes later, a beautiful 25 yard volley from Jonathan Wright into the top right hand corner of the net gave Blackhouse no chance. I said to Robbo that this should be an easy victory for Stan, maybe 6-0, but I was to seriously eat my words. Uni suddenly woke up and for the rest of the first half played some pacey, positive, attacking football and began to threaten. Lee Scott pulled one back for them just before half time.

Uni started the second half in a confident manner and equalised on 54 minutes when Joe Robertson prodded the ball home after a bit of a goalmouth scramble. While Uni were gaining in confidence, Stan seemed to lose the plot a bit. Even so, with 10 minutes remaining, after Uni's Niza Chilufya hit the post, Stan quickly moved the ball up the pitch and Ross Thirlaway's shot produced a good save from Blackhouse. The winner came in the 85th minute – Chris Scott smashing the ball home – to complete a great comeback from the Northern League newcomers. A late scare in time added on when Uni's Adam Redford cleared Stan's Thibault Charmey's shot off the goal line would have been cruel on Uni, who I thought overall deserved the win, mainly due to their sheer dogged determination after that nightmare start. As for Stan, they were taught a bit of a lesson by the Uni tonight. After two games and two defeats, their Report Card reads 'must do better'.

Vital Statistics:

Newcastle University 3 (Lee Scott 45, Joe Robertson 54, Chris Scott 85)

Heaton Stannington 2 (Paterson 3, Wright 5)

At Kimberley Park, Prudhoe, Northumberland

Northern League Division 2

Admission £4

Programme £1

Attendance 154

WINDY TOWN

Northern League Ground 24

Saturday 17th August 2019
BILLINGHAM TOWN
Bedford Terrace, Billingham, Cleveland

Founded in 1967 as Billingham Social. Played in and won the Stockton and District League and Teesside League. In 1982, changed name to Billingham Town and joined Northern League Division 2. Promoted to Division 1 in 1984/85 but relegated in 1985/86. Promoted again 1987/88 but relegated again 1989/90. Promoted 1996/97 until 2013/14 when they were relegated back to Division 2. Promoted as Division 2 champions in 2018/19.

Northern League Cup winners 2007/08

Durham Challenge Cup winners 2003/04

Best FA Cup performance – 4th Qualifying Round 2000/01

Best FA Vase performance – 5th Round 1997/98

The singer/songwriter/guitarist Chris Rea comes from this general neck of the woods, and one of his songs – Windy Town – would have been very apt to describe my visit to Billingham Town's match against Ashington today. The beautiful sunny afternoon would have been perfect weather for watching football if there had not been winds of up to 20 mph to accompany the sunshine. Right from the kick off it was clear that both teams were going to be playing against the wind as well as each other. Billingham (or Billy as their fans call them) started brightly, laying siege to the Ashington goalmouth that I was standing behind on the grass terrace. In the first ten minutes, I retrieved the ball twice from behind the goal, both times sending slick accurate right foot passes to the Billy player moving over to take the corner. I was pleased with my skills, and at this point, I had touched the ball more than Billy's keeper.

Billingham Town nearly folded in February 2018 but have seen a remarkable turnaround both on and off the field since then, culminating in their promotion to Division 1 as last season's Division 2 champions. Lottery funding has enabled them to carry out improvements to the changing rooms and officials room, with the clubhouse presently being refurbished. Like Ashington they had started this season's league campaign with a win and two losses. Their two defeats had both been at home so their fervent fans were hoping for a change of fortune today. They hit the bar on 15 minutes and just before half time Elliott Beddow should have scored when one on one with Ashington keeper Daniel Staples but he fluffed his lines. The wind was the winner in a goalless first half.

After refuelling on beer and pies at the interval, the Billy faithful were soon celebrating (I spotted some 'dad dancing' in the main stand) when their striker Kallum Hannah scored two minutes into the second half. After this Ashington enjoyed their best spell in the match so far. On the hour mark, their keeper Staples nearly beat Billy keeper Brad Young with a great (possibly wind assisted) kick from his own penalty area, and minutes later they equalised when Billy's James Frazer put the ball into his own net. One of their fans on Twitter described it as 'a quality finish' and another tweeted 'he had a great game today and deserved a goal'. Top banter. Minutes later Billy were back in front via a cool finish from Craig Hutchinson (last season's Division 2 Golden Boot winner with 43 goals). On 70 minutes the visitors made a triple substitution. The fresh legs made a difference with Ashington in the ascendency and twice going close to drawing level again. The home side saw the game out however and on the balance of play I reckon just about deserved their first home league win of the season.

Vital Statistics:

Billingham Town 2 (Hannah 47, Hutchinson 64)

Ashington 1 (Frazer og 62)

Northern League Division 1

Admission £6,

Programme £1

Attendance 190

SCORCHIO IN NORTHALLERTON
Northern League Ground 25

Monday 26th August 2019
NORTHALERTON TOWN
The Calvert Stadium, Ainderby Road, Romanby, Northallerton, North Yorkshire.

Generally accepted that they formed in 1895. Have been known as Northallerton, Northallerton Alliance and Northallerton Town, and played in various local leagues. In 1982 joined Northern League Division 2, and promoted to Division 1 in 1989/90. Relegated 1994/95, promoted again 1996/97 but relegated again 1997/98. Promoted 2005/06, relegated 2008/09 and promoted 2018/19.

Northern League Division 2 champions 1996/97

Best FA Cup performance – 4th Qualifying Round 1992/93, 1993/94

Best FA Vase performance – 4th Round 2002/03

On a day that weather presenter Paula Fisch on the classic TV comedy The Fast Show would certainly describe as 'scorchio!' and UK news media were reporting as the hottest day since 1066 (or something like that), Anita and I drove down the A1 for the early (11 am) Bank Holiday match between Northallerton Town and their local North Yorkshire rivals Guisborough Town.

On arrival we received a very friendly welcome from the club volunteers selling raffle tickets and handing out team sheets. The match programmes had sold out but the team sheet man, clearly sensing my extreme disappointment, very kindly sold me his at the £1.50 face value. (I have a programme from all the Northern League matches I have attended, and yes I own an anorak). Newly promoted Northallerton have had a tough start to life in Division 1. They have lost 3 and won 1 of their first 4 matches. In contrast, Guisborough have made a good start, winning 3 and losing 1 of their first 4 games.

Today's match followed the form book, when after a competitive first 15 minutes (Northallerton missed a glorious chance on 7 minutes), the visitors by and large controlled the proceedings for the rest of the game. They opened the scoring on 34 minutes – Danny Earl heading home from Steven Snaith's free kick. Their second goal on 53 minutes was a beauty – a first time shot from Lewis Hawkins into the bottom corner of the net after some skilful dribbling on the right from substitute John Howard. Five minutes later they rattled the Northallerton bar and were awarded a penalty when a foul was committed in the ensuing goalmouth scramble. Captain Mark Robinson made no mistake from the spot to seal the win. Northallerton were awarded a penalty on 78 minutes but James Rowe's spot kick was saved by Ryan Catterick diving down to his right hand side.

The missed penalty seemed to sum up Northallerton's day. They huffed and puffed but did not really threaten, and I feel they ran out of steam as the second half progressed. This was their second 3-0 home defeat in 3 days (they lost to Stockton in the FA Cup). On today's evidence, they will have a testing season at this higher level but Anita and I thoroughly enjoyed this visit to their picturesque ground with their friendly supporters. We wished them all the best for the rest of the campaign.

Ladies' toilet report – contrary to what some people might think, I do not spend my time visiting ladies' toilets at non-league grounds. It is fair to say that many grounds at this level have some poor facilities for females, but Anita reliably informed me that Northallerton Town FC is not one of them. The ladies was very clean and tidy, with photos of Bob Marley and Audrey Hepburn on one wall, and Marilyn Monroe wallpaper on another wall! She gave it an 8 out of 10.

Vital Statistics:

Northallerton Town 0

Guisborough Town 3 (Earl 34, Hawkins 53, Robinson 58 pen)

Northern League Division 1

Admission £6

Programme £1.50

Attendance 244

ONLY FOODS AND SAUCES
Northern League Ground 26

Saturday 31st August 2019
CROOK TOWN
Sir Tom Cowie Millfield Ground, West Road, Crook, County Durham

Founded in 1889. Joined the Bishop Auckland and District League in 1894 and the Northern League in 1896. Won FA Amateur Cup for the first time in 1901. In 1945, after the Second World War, Northern League resumed and they re-joined the league as Crook Colliery Welfare. In 1949 changed name to Crook Town again. Won the FA Amateur Cup 4 times in an 11 year period (1954, 1959, 1962, 1964). Nicknamed The Black and Ambers.

Northern League champions 1914/15, 1926/27, 1952/53, 1958/59, 1962/63

Northern League Division 2 champions 2012/13

Northern League Cup winners 1936/37, 1945/46, 1960/61

Durham Challenge Cup winners 1926/27, 1931/32, 1954/55, 1959/60

Best FA Cup performance – 3rd Round 1931/32

Best FA Trophy performance – 3rd Round 1976/77

Best FA vase performance – Quarter Final 2005/06

In the week that saw Bury FC, a club with a 134 year history, sadly expelled from the English Football League due to unpaid debts and poor management, a first time visit to Crook Town, a club with a similar lengthy history seemed appropriate. Unlike Bury, who played in the Football League for 125 years, Crook have always been a non-league club but have enjoyed some glory years at that level, particularly the FA Amateur Cup wins in the 1950s and 1960s. Today they were playing in the 1st Qualifying Round of the FA Vase, the competition that effectively replaced the FA Amateur Cup when it was scrapped in 1974. This seemed to me to be another appropriate reason to visit Crook Town today.

The Football Association Challenge Vase (to give it its full title) is competed for by clubs below Level 8 of the English Football Pyramid. Crook's Road To Wembley (the Final is scheduled to take place there in May 2020) started with a home tie against their fellow Northern League Division 2 local rivals Brandon United.

On arriving at The Sir Tom Cowie Millfield Ground, I seriously thought I was stepping back in time – in a good way. This is one of the very best Northern League grounds I have visited. It has 2 lovely old-style traditional stands next to each other on one side of the pitch (one built in 1925 has permanently fixed seats, and one is covered terracing with plastic chairs on the back row). There is a standing terrace with crush barriers behind one goal, that reminded me a bit of the Gallowgate End at St James Park, Newcastle in 1970s (without the rank smell of the outside toilets though), and there are grass banks behind the other goal and on the other side of the pitch opposite the 2 stands. In the 1950s, gates of 10,000 were the norm for Cup matches here (17,000 being the highest recorded crowd). The crowd was 137 today.

The match was an entertaining affair. Daniel Kent gave Crook an early lead after 4 minutes, slotting the ball past the advancing Brandon keeper Carl Robinson. Matthew Lovegreen grabbed the visitors' equaliser on 24 minutes. The second half was a proper cup tie that seemed to be heading towards extra time until Crook's Christian Holliday headed the winning goal into the bottom corner with 4 minutes remaining.

But why the heading Only Foods and Sauces you may (or may not) be asking? Well, it is the name of the hot food and drink snack bar in the ground (I bought a very palatable burger from it for £2). It has the accolade of being my new favourite named food outlet on my groundhopping travels so far (it has just pipped Ryton & Crawcrook Albion's The Scran Van). Seasoned groundhoppers will understand the importance of rating these things. Maybe I am now becoming more groundhopper-ish?

Like Bury, Crook Town have also flirted with going out of business (in the 2015/16 season). They survived but like several teams at this level they are finding things tough financially. I hope they continue their proud 130 year history and I will certainly be revisiting this great ground again sometime.

Vital Statistics:

Crook Town 2 (Kent 4, Holliday 86)

Brandon United 1 (Lovegreen 24)

FA Vase 1st Qualifying Round

Admission £5

Programme £1

Attendance 137

BESIDE THE SEASIDE
Northern League Ground 27

Saturday 7th September 2019
REDCAR ATHLETIC
Green Lane, Redcar, Teesside

Established in 1993 as Teesside Athletic and played in the Teesside League. Joined the Wearside League in 2005. Changed name to Redcar Athletic in 2010. Gained promotion to Northern League Division 2 at end of 2017/18 season as Wearside League champions. Nicknamed The Steelmen.

FA Community Club of the Year 2005 and 2007

On arriving at this seaside town after an hour's drive from Newcastle, Anita and I were left in no doubt that the summer holiday season here was over. We parked on the sea front and as soon as we got out of the car we were hit with an extremely cold wind blowing in from the North Sea. We nipped into a café, partly to shelter and partly to order from the all-day breakfast menu (and very good it was too).

Redcar Athletic's Green Lane ground is near to the coast and we felt the chill a bit at their match with Crook Town today. The ground has a very well appointed clubhouse and there are some improvements to the areas around the pitch taking place. The Steelmen have made an unbeaten start to what is only their second season in the Northern League, winning 5 and drawing 2 of their first 7 matches. They are currently sitting 3rd in Division 2, with Crook close behind them in 7th place. We sat in the stand which at least provided a small amount of shelter from the wind.

Before kick-off there was a minute's applause for Jimmy Rowe, the Newcastle Benfield FC Chairman who had sadly passed away during the week. This is another great example of the camaraderie that exists between the clubs at this level. For all their rivalries on the pitch, I have found during my Northern League groundhopping that there is a great deal of mutual respect and friendship amongst clubs away from the pitch. There was a large travelling support from Crook today, contributing to make it the highest crowd of the season so far at Green Lane.

There was a cagey start to the match. The first real chance fell to Crook's Daniel Kent after 15 minutes but Redcar's keeper Ollie Simpson pushed his low shot around the post. After 20 minutes Crook's Chris Dickinson missed a glorious chance, firing wide with Simpson beaten. Against the run of play, The Steelmen took the lead just before half time when Jordan Rivis' free kick took a wicked deflection and wrong footed Crook keeper Ronan Makepeace. In the second half, both sides played open attacking football. Crook hit the Redcar crossbar twice in search of the equaliser, and both keepers made crucial saves. The Steelmen sealed the win on 81 minutes through a Lee Bythway header. In the dying minutes, Crook's Jake Petitjean was shown a red card for stamping on Chris Bivens.

We felt Crook were unfortunate not to go home with something out of a very open and entertaining match. Apart from the defeat, their fans seemed to enjoy their day at the seaside – even their elderly supporter standing behind the goal who was knocked out by an off target rocket shot (he made a full recovery after some treatment from the physio). As for Redcar, they were well organised, very solid defensively and look like promotion contenders.

Vital Statistics:

Redcar Athletic 2 (Rivis 37, Bythway 81) Crook Town 0
Northern League Division 2
Admission £5
Programme £1
Attendance 201
.......SECOND MISSION......MAKING GOOD PROGRESS......

ALL BRAN? NO, MAINLY STAN

Northern League Ground 28

Saturday 14th September 2019
BRANDON UNITED
Welfare Ground, Rear Commercial Street, Brandon, County Durham

Originally formed as a Sunday morning works team called Rostrons and played in the Durham and District Sunday League. Joined the Northern Alliance in 1977. After one season (1980/81) in the Northern Amateur League they joined the Wearside League. Moved up to Northern League Division 2 for 1983/84 season. Promoted to Division 1 at end of 1984/85 season. Relegated to Division 2 (1993/94), promoted back to Division 1 (1999/2000) but relegated back to Division 2 (2005/06).

Northern League Division 1 champions 2002/03

Best FA Cup performance - 1st Round 1979/80, 1988/89

Best FA Vase performance – Quarter Final 1982/83, 1983/84

I drove to Brandon (just west of the city of Durham) with Robbo. As previously stated, he is first and foremost a Sunderland FC supporter (season ticket holder). Sunderland were playing away today so he jumped at the chance to travel to watch his local non-league team Heaton Stannington (Brandon United's opponents today). This was, in fact, the third time he had watched The Stan in the last 8 days (he was at their home games v Tow Law last Saturday and v Billingham Synthonia on Wednesday night) and he freely admitted it was currently more entertaining watching them than watching Sunderland. He was not the only Stan fan who had made the journey from Tyneside to The Land of the Prince Bishops today. We stood with the dozen or so travelling diehards, including Harry The Dog (the club mascot who has his own Twitter page with more followers than most humans have – 485 at the time of writing – he is 'a mud connoisseur, expert retriever of cricket balls and cheeky charmer of the ladies!').

Brandon United are currently 2nd bottom of Northern League Division 2 with only 1 win from 7 so far, but Heaton Stannington are only 5 places higher after making another characteristic slow start to the season. The pitch looked in good condition and it was a sunny day, but Brandon's elevated location and the open aspect of the ground (three sides are very exposed to the elements) meant the wind played its part in the match today.

An early goal for Stan (Thibault Charmey coolly slotting Jon Wright's cross home from 12 yards) set the tone for the first half. Brandon's players immediately started arguing amongst themselves and the F-word seemed to be the most commonly used word as the game progressed. Stan were playing the better football and when Charmey scored his second after 23 minutes from a Wright corner it looked like game over unless Brandon got their heads back up. Charmey should have completed his hat trick on 33 minutes when he rounded the Brandon keeper but somehow fired his shot wide of an open goal (incredibly, he did the same thing again in the second half). Stan were well on top and their 2 -0 interval lead could have been much more.

The Brandon half time team talk had an early positive effect, when they pulled a goal back after 50 minutes – Lewis Martin in space, shooting into the top of the net (Robbo and I missed this goal as we were still in the clubhouse). The home side went in search of the equaliser as the wind grew stronger, making accurate passing more difficult. This was Brandon's best spell of the match but they were soon back to arguing and swearing again when Stan's Daniel Sayer broke through their defence and slipped the ball into the far corner of the net. Stan's 4th goal from Jordan Ray on 76 minutes sealed a convincing win.

All in all, a good day out at Brandon United. The club has seen better times (their finest hour was 2002/03 when they won Northern League Division 1) and they have flirted with relegation from Division 2 for the last few seasons. There is certainly some fight in them though (they had drawn their last 2 league matches prior to today) but they look likely to be involved in another relegation battle this season. As for Heaton Stannington, they have some decent young players and are showing some signs of improvement. Robbo, Harry and the others were hoping that this was the start of a good run and a climb up the league table.

Vital Statistics:

Brandon United 1 (Martin 50)

Heaton Stannington 4 (Charmey 3, 23, Sayer 64, Ray 76)

Northern League Division 2

Admission £5

Programme £1

Attendance - circa 60 (rough head count)

"THERE'S ONLY ONE TEAM IN BIRTLEY!"
Northern League Ground 29

Tuesday 1st October 2019
BIRTLEY TOWN
Birtley Sports Complex, Durham Road, Birtley, Tyne and Wear

The original Birtley FC played in the inaugural 1889/90 Northern League season, finished 2nd bottom and joined the Northern Alliance the following season. From 1926 they played in the North Eastern League, then joined the Wearside League in 1935. After the Second World War, changed name to Birtley Town. Folded in 1952.

Reformed in 1992 and re-joined the Wearside League. Champions in 2002/03 and 2006/07 – promoted to Northern League Division 2 for 2007/08 season. At end of 2015/16 season they were relegated to Northern Alliance but were promoted back to Northern League Division 2 at end of 2017/18 season. Nicknamed The Hoops.

…. or at least that is how it felt on this miserable Tuesday night when Birtley Town faced Hebburn Town in a Northern League Cup match. Even allowing for the fact that the teams are a league apart (prior to kick-off Hebburn were top of Northern League Division 1 and Birtley were 4th in Division 2) no one could have predicted how one-sided this turned out tonight. For those old enough to remember the teleprinter churning out the football scores at 4.50 pm on Saturdays on Grandstand on BBC TV, tonight's result would have been presented as Birtley Town 0 Hebburn Town 13 (Thirteen) i.e. the word 'Thirteen' shown in brackets after the number '13' to avoid any doubt or disbelief in the score.

I attended the match with David Cruise– a new travelling companion making his Northern League debut. We have known each other for about 50 years. We both lived and grew up in what are affectionately known as The Avenues in Gateshead. Back in those days, we would have probably thought it unlikely that half a century later we would be meeting on a cold damp October night to watch non-league football in Birtley but, after having pre-match pints in nearby Low Fell and cans of Guinness in the clubhouse, here we were. David was a very keen trainspotter in his youth and still has an interest in train related stuff. With the East Coast mainline running near to the ground, trains were whizzing past every five minutes and I was a bit worried that they would distract him from the football ('once a trainspotter always a trainspotter?') but he managed to control himself.

As for the match, to be blunt, Birtley Town were completely outplayed by

Hebburn Town. The visitors opened the scoring after 5 minutes via Carl Taylor's delightful curling shot into the top right corner of the net from about 25 yards out. Oliver Martin added a second and third on 10 and 24 minutes and when Luke Sullivan scored their fourth after 29 minutes (the first of his 4 goals) the match was effectively over as a contest. It was a night to forget for Birtley (their PA announcer was becoming more and more despondent as he read out the Hebburn goalscorers) but Hebburn did not let up, playing a very slick passing game with maximum effort. I will spare Birtley's blushes further by simply saying it was 6-0 at half time and 13-0 at full time. They have made a steady start in Division 2 this season and need to just put this defeat behind them. Hebburn look like serious contenders for the Division 1 title. They broke 3 club records tonight – the most goals scored in a game, biggest ever margin of victory and 7 different goalscorers in one game. Talking of records, David and I agreed that this was the most one-sided match either of us had ever witnessed.

Vital Statistics:

Birtley Town 0 Hebburn Town 13 (Taylor 5, Martin 10, 24, Sullivan 29, 44, 52, 86, Richardson 35, 79, Suddick 55, Storey 60, 83, Dibb-Fuller 89)

Mitre Brooks Mileson Northern League Cup (Group H)

Admission £5

Programme – none (we were told there was a problem at the printers but we were given half a dozen old Birtley Town programmes each by a club volunteer.... just when we are both trying to kick the programme collecting habit)

Attendance 142

SHELTERED LIFE
Northern League Ground 30

Saturday 5th October 2019
ESH WINNING
West Terrace, Waterhouses, Esh Winning, County Durham

Founded in 1889 as Esh Winning Rangers. Joined the Northern League in 1912 and won the league in their first season. Folded in 1934 due to financial difficulties.

Re-formed in 1969 as Esh Winning Pineapple, playing in Durham and District Sunday League. Promoted to Northern Alliance in 1981. In 1982, dropped Pineapple from their name and joined Northern League Division 2. Nicknamed The Stags.

Best FA Cup performance – 2nd Qualifying Round 1990/91, 2004/05

Best FA Vase performance – 2nd Round 1983/84, 1992/93, 2001/02, 2004/05, 2012/13

My brother Kev was visiting the North East for the weekend and he accompanied me to the former colliery village of Esh Winning today. 'Esh' is the Saxon word for Ash, and 'Winning' was a Victorian term used when coal was found. Esh's West Terrace ground meets all the criteria for grounds at Level 10 of the English Football League pyramid structure (e.g. covered stand with acceptable number of seats, clubhouse facilities, permanently fixed pitch barrier). It also has however, what I am sure must be, a fairly unique set up of 4 old bus shelters at the side of the pitch opposite the clubhouse, and 2 wooden shelters and some wooden park benches at the top of the grassed terracing behind one of the goals. There were some older gentlemen diehard supporters occupying the wooden shelters, who will surely have witnessed many up and downs during, in the football sense, their sheltered life.

Since joining the Northern League, Esh have spent most of the time in the lower reaches of Division 2. They did however have highs of 2 spells totalling 6 seasons in Division 1 in the early part of the 21st Century, and won the Ernest Armstrong Memorial Cup (competed for by teams in Northern League Division 2) in 2007/08 season without conceding a single goal in the 4 matches. These old gents in their shelters have endured another frustrating start to this season. Esh have only 1 win from 10 matches in the league, are sitting in the bottom 3, and last weekend surrendered a 2 goal lead to lose 4-2 at home to bottom club Durham City.

In contrast, today's visitors West Allotment Celtic have had a great start to the season. They are 2nd top of the league with 8 wins from 10 matches and have progressed to the First Round Proper of the FA Vase after 2 emphatic away wins in the qualifying rounds. The sides were meeting today for the second time this week – Allotment beat Esh 2-0 in midweek on their Druid Park home turf in the Northern League Cup. The gap in league positions was not obvious in the first half though, with Esh matching Allotment for endeavour. It was goalless at half time, and the home side could perhaps count themselves unfortunate not to be ahead after forcing 2 good saves from Allotment keeper Finlay Hodgson. After the break, Allotment moved up a gear and striker Matty Hayton opened the scoring just two minutes into the second half. Kev missed this goal (toilet break) and when he came back I stopped myself from saying 'Esh Winning are losing' because it did not seem very original (I am sure it has been said many times before and certainly many times so far this season). Hayton went on to score a hat trick with Esh finding it increasingly difficult as the match progressed to deal with Allotment's attacking threat. Mikel Thompson added a late fourth goal to complete another good away win for the visitors. The comedy moment of the day occurred in the 65th minute when an Allotment player inexplicably appealed for a penalty after Esh keeper Craig Hannant palmed away a shot. Overall, we thought it was an entertaining match at a very friendly club in a quirky little ground in a picturesque location (what more could you want at this level of football). It was also a fairly mild and dry day for early October, so even though there were plenty of places to shelter in the ground, they were not required today.

Vital Statistics:

Esh Winning 0 West Allotment Celtic 4 (Hayton 47, 69, 88, Thompson 90)

Northern League Division 2

Admission £5,

Programme £1

Attendance 61

CLOSE CONTEST IN CHILLY CARLISLE
Northern League Ground 31

Saturday 19th October 2019
CARLISLE CITY
Gillford Park Stadium, Carlisle, Cumbria

Formed in 1975 by 2 ex-Carlisle United players (Ron Thompson and George Walker) to give local lads somewhere to play. Joined the Northern Alliance. Relegated to Northern Combination League at end of 1986/87 season. At the end of the 1987/88 season, the Northern Combination merged into the Northern Alliance and they re-joined Division 1 of the Alliance. Champions in 1991/92 and promoted to the Premier Division of the Alliance. At end of 2015/16 season, gained promotion to Division 1 of North West Counties League. At end of 2018/19 season they were transferred to Northern League Division 2. Nicknamed The Sky Blues.

Best FA Cup performance – 1st Qualifying Round 1976/77, 1977/78, 1978/79, 1979/80

Best FA Vase performance – 3rd Round 1976/77

I decided to tick off Carlisle City FC's ground today. It was the farthest away of the grounds still to visit on The Second Mission – approximately 60 miles from Newcastle. I thought it would be better to do this sooner rather than later, and well before the unpredictable Cumbrian Winter arrives. Anita accompanied me to the match. This required a little bit of bribery of course – i.e. an overnight hotel stop and a very tasty steak dinner in nearby Cockermouth.

Carlisle City's Gillford Park ground is located just south east of Carlisle town centre. Its capacity is 4,000 with a large stand behind the dugouts, a smaller stand with clubhouse behind one goal (next to the main West Coast railway line) and a covered standing area along the side of the pitch opposite the dugouts. There was a mobile food van (The Little Griddle) next to the smaller stand offering, amongst other delicacies, Cumberland sausage and black pudding in a bun. It looked great but we had already had the Unlimited Breakfast at the Premier Inn in Cockermouth that morning, so we decided on the sensible healthy option, settled for a cup of tea and took our seats in the large stand.

City's opponents today were Sunderland West End. Both clubs are enjoying their first season in the Northern League – City were transferred from the North West Counties League Division One North, and West End were promoted from the Wearside League. Before kick-off, the PA Announcer welcomed the West End players, officials and fans (there were a couple of dozen hardy souls who had made the trip from Sunderland) and said he thought it was the first time the sides had ever met...but he couldn't be absolutely certain....but he reckoned it was.... possibly...maybe. They have both made a reasonable start to life in this new league, and pre-kick off they were both currently sitting in the fairly tight mid-table area of Division 2 (City 10th with 18 points and West End 15th with 15 points).

It was a dull, dreary, cold day. There had been a bit of overnight rain and it had also rained constantly for two hours before kick-off, meaning the pitch quickly started cutting up when the action started. The match turned out to be an actual Game of Two Halves. City opened the scoring after 7 minutes when Jordan Palmer's great 25 yard shot whizzed past West End keeper Neal Bussey, hit the bar, then hit Bussey's back and finished up in the net. The home side controlled the first half and 2 goals by Robert McCartney around the half hour mark gave them a 3-0 half time lead.

West End started the second half brightly and almost scored straight from the re-start. Their pressure paid off after 55 minutes when Daniel Martin pulled a goal back for them. City were suddenly on the back foot as West End pressed to get back into the match. The visitors twice went close to scoring a crucial second goal on 60 and 63 minutes. However, on 74 minutes a weak kick from Bussey fell to City striker Marc Shiel who rounded Bussey and scored City's fourth goal. This looked like a fatal blow to West End's comeback hopes, but their spirited and improved second half performance continued, and after 79 minutes it was 4-2 after a mix-up in the City defence. The home fans were on edge now and had to endure 4 nervous minutes of additional time when on 90 minutes West End's Kieron Beattie reduced the deficit to 4-3. A late penalty claim was turned down and met with fury from the Away dugout, but City held on for the narrow win that moved them up to 6th in the table. West End dropped to 16th but with 6 points separating them from 4th place, if they can play like they did in the second half and not like they did in the first half, the only way will be up not down.

Vital Statistics:

Carlisle City 4 (Palmer 7, McCartney 26, 32, Shiel 74)

Sunderland West End 3 (Martin 55, Old 79, Beattie 90)

Northern League Division 2

Admission £4

Programme £1

Attendance 85

.....SECOND MISSION......AT HALFWAY STAGE.......

THE CUMBRIAN CELTIC

Tuesday 5th November 2019
Cleator Moor Celtic versus Crown Newlaithes
McGrath Park, Cleator Moor, Cumbria

Anita and I were having a few days break on the West Cumbrian coast when I noticed there was an opportunity to tick off a new ground in the area. After some hillwalking during the day (we reached the summit of Dodd in the Bassenthwaite area – height 1,612 feet) we decided to travel to Cleator Moor Celtic FC for their Cumberland Senior Cup tie with Carlisle-based Crown Newlaithes FC. Actually saying we decided is not strictly true. It would be more accurate to say I decided and dragged Anita along. It was a 7.30 pm kick off but after some minor route finding difficulties on B roads (by me I would add) we arrived 10 minutes late. We then realised we were parked on the wrong side of the ground so after a bit of walking around the nearby streets we eventually entered the ground at 7.45 pm (it was still goalless).

We sat in the small covered stand that had 4 rows of 10 seats in the green and white club colours. Cleator Moor Celtic play in the North West Counties League Division 1 North (Step 6 of the non-league pyramid). Crown Newlaithes play at a lower level in the Cumberland County League but in the half hour of the first half that we saw they more than matched their higher league hosts. It remained goalless at half time. Anita was distracted from the action at times – watching the boxer dog in the row in front of us instead (this is quite normal behaviour for her). We got cups of tea during the interval and it is worth giving Cleator Moor Celtic FC an honorary mention of being the only club I have visited so far that serve tea in proper china mugs (not the usual Styrofoam ones). They also allowed us to take them out of the clubhouse and drink them in the stand (5 star service).

Crown started the second half brightly and after 55 minutes had their best chance of the match, forcing a great save from the Celtic keeper. They then opened the scoring on 63 minutes (their Twitter page confirmed the scorer was Luke Firth). A minute later Celtic equalised via a cracking shot from the left side edge of the penalty area. On 70 minutes the visitors missed a good chance to re-take the lead, and 2 minutes later it was Celtic who took the lead with a scrambled second goal. Celtic wasted a good chance to wrap it up on 77 minutes but held out anyway to clinch a place in the quarter final after a very entertaining open cup tie. Given it was bonfire night, the game was played against a backdrop of fireworks going off in the nearby streets throughout. Whenever a firework exploded into the night sky, the boxer dog barked at it – he ain't afraid of no firework!

Back at home 2 days later, we watched Glasgow Celtic beat Lazio on TV in the Europa League. They also won 2-1 via a dramatic injury time winner to qualify for the knock out stages. It would be hard to argue that our trip to the Cumbrian Celtic of Cleator Moor eclipsed the actual Celtic fans euphoric trip to Rome. It was however an enjoyable evening and well worth the effort (Anita only partially agrees with this).

Vital Statistics:

Cleator Moor Celtic 2 Crown Newlaithes 1

Cumberland Senior Cup 2nd Round

Admission £2

Programme – none left when we arrived
(but the club very kindly posted one to me later)

Attendance - circa 70 (rough estimate)

CHAPTER

MOVING THE GOALPOSTS
(UNFINISHED BUSINESS)
AROUND THE NORTHERN LEAGUE GROUNDS

(Part 4 – December 2019 to March 2020)

THORNABY TRIP RECOMPLETES NORTHERN LEAGUE DIVISION 1
Northern League Ground 32

Saturday 7th December 2019
THORNABY
Teesdale Park, Acklam Road, Thornaby, Stockton-on-Tees

Formed in 1980 as Stockton FC and played in the Wearside League. Joined the Northern League in 1985. Changed name to Thornaby-on-Tees FC in 1999 and to Thornaby FC the next season. Nicknamed The Blues or The Teessiders

Northern League Division 2 champions 1987/88, 1991/92

After a frustrating November, when all the Northern League games I had planned to attend were postponed due to waterlogged pitches, I returned to my groundhopping Mission today with a visit to Thornaby FC. As previously outlined, I ticked off all the Northern League Division 1 grounds last season. The unwritten, but widely understood and accepted, rules of groundhopping meant that to recomplete this league (groundhopper-speak) I needed to attend matches at the grounds of the 3 teams promoted from last season's Division 2. In August I ticked off Billingham Town and Northallerton Town and this trip to Thornaby (the last of the 3 promoted teams) recompleted the Division 1.

The weather on Teesside was as good as it gets for early December – clear and dry, not too cold. The normally very reliable Futbology App on my phone suggested that I parked near to the ground, followed by what seemed to be a short 2 minute walk to it through the nearby cemetery. I entered and walked through the cemetery, but although I could see the floodlights of the football ground at its far end, there was no exit. (I suppose this is the very way cemeteries operate – there is a way in but no way out). I retraced my steps and after a slightly longer walk around the outside of the cemetery along a lane full of small potholes, I made it to the ground just before kick-off.

Thornaby were currently lying 3rd bottom of the league, 2 places and 3 points above today's opponents Whickham, and with both teams on poor runs of form, even at the mid-season stage this match felt like the proverbial six-pointer relegation clash. Whickham had recently appointed former Newcastle United and Norwich City veteran midfielder Matty Pattison as player-manager, with John Oster (ex-Everton, Sunderland and Wales) as his assistant. Both had spells at Gateshead later in their playing careers. Pattison was playing for Whickham today, with Oster shouting encouragement and instructions from the dugout. The opening period was pretty even with both teams having half chances. It was Whickham who opened the scoring after 22 minutes through Jonny Burn's strike after a good cross from Pattison. Thornaby had a good 10 minute spell after the goal but the visitors defended stoutly, including a great double save from keeper Jack Wilson on 32 minutes. Shortly before half time Whickham went close to increasing their lead with efforts from Carl Finnigan and Pattison, but it remained 1-0 at the break.

During half time I had a wander around the stadium, and very quirky it is too. The main Peter Morris Stand on the dugouts side of the pitch houses the Thornaby Blue Army. On the opposite side of the pitch there is an old bus shelter at the halfway line that some Whickham fans were standing in and around. Behind one goal there is a covered cowshed type standing area with a corrugated iron roof, and behind the other goal there is the clubhouse and a newly built untreated wooden roofless stand with blue plastic seats (I am guessing this was built after they clinched promotion from Division 2).

Thornaby started the second half brightly and their striker Adam Preston twice went close to scoring on 47 and 50 minutes. Whickham then went close twice – Tom Howard had a shot cleared off the line on 53 minutes, and on the hour mark Max Cowburn just failed to get enough on the ball in front of goal. The visitors were now taking control of the game and they made it 2-0 on 71 minutes when another good cross from Pattison was not dealt with by the Thornaby defence and Cowburn fired the ball home. Whickham saw the game out in a professional manner and their new management team must have been very pleased with the away win and a clean sheet. In comparison, the Thornaby fans near to me were definitely not pleased with their team's overall effort today. The result meant Whickham moved up to 2nd bottom on the same points as Thornaby but with a slightly inferior goal difference.

Vital statistics

Thornaby 0 Whickham 2 (Burn 22, Cowburn 71)
Northern League Division 1
Admission £6
Programme £1.50
Attendance 90

WESTEND GOALS
Northern League Ground 33

Saturday 21st December 2019
SUNDERLAND WEST END
Nissan Sports Complex, Washington Road, Sunderland, Tyne and Wear

Original incarnation of the club played in the Wearside League from 1892/93 season until 1929/30 season.

Current club was formed in 2006 as Jolly Potter, then changed name to Houghton Town. Played in Wearside Combination League. In 2011 changed name to Sunderland West End and joined the Wearside League again (after an 81 year gap). Finished runners-up in Wearside League in 2018/19 and were promoted to Northern League Division 2

On the last busy shopping Saturday before Christmas there is no place I would rather be than at a football match. My mate Dekka felt the same, so we headed in the opposite direction of the shoppers at Gateshead MetroCentre and Newcastle Eldon Square to the Nissan Sports Complex – the temporary home of Sunderland West End FC. As previously stated, Dekka has a season ticket for another team in Sunderland (the one that plays in Level 3 of the English Football Pyramid) but they did not have a match today so he took the opportunity to support his favourite non-league team – Ryton and Crawcrook Albion (aka RACA), West End's opponents today. He has been to a few RACA home games this season and pre-match we had good craic in the clubhouse with some of RACA's fans who he knew (including Kit Man Don McCloud and Club Secretary Kev Wilkinson). West End are struggling a bit in their first season in the Northern League (currently 5th bottom) while RACA have had a good season so far (currently 4th top).

There was nothing between the sides in the first period of the first half, but when Sam Norris opened the scoring for RACA on 27 minutes with a cracking strike they started to take control of the game. After 43 minutes Norris grabbed his second goal with a good chipped finish and a minute later Scott Jasper made it 3-0 at half time. It felt like they had already put the game to bed.

In the second half, West End never gave up trying and went close a couple of times but overall RACA continued to dominate, with wave upon wave of attacks. Three more goals (a 25 yard drive from Jack Cooper, a close range shot from substitute Matty Slee, and a Sam Norris penalty to complete his hat trick) made it a comfortable, comprehensive 6-0 victory and RACA moved up to 3rd in the table. Sadly not much Christmas cheer for Sunderland West End though, who look likely to be scrapping at the other end of the table for the rest of the season.

Vital Statistics:

Sunderland West End 0

Ryton and Crawcrook Albion 6 (Norris 27, 43, 86 pen, Jasper 44, Cooper 71, Slee 82)

Northern League Division 2

Admission £5

Programme – none

Attendance 60

COLLIERS' COMEBACK
Northern League Ground 34

Saturday 28th December 2019
EASINGTON COLLIERY
Welfare Park, Memorial Avenue, Easington, County Durham

Formed in 1913 and played in the Wearside League. Changed name to Easington Colliery Welfare in 1919. Disbanded in 1964 but reformed and re-joined the Wearside League in 1973. Dropped Welfare from their name in 1976. Joined Northern League Division 2 in 1985 and were promoted to Division 1 at the end of their first season. Relegated back to Division 2 (1989/90), promoted back to Division 1 (1990/91), relegated again (1992/93), promoted again (1995/96), and relegated again (2000/01). In 2004/05 they were relegated to the Northern Alliance, and in 2006/07 they transferred to the Wearside League. Promoted to Northern League Division 2 in 2014/15.

Best FA Cup performance – 1st round 1955/56

Best FA Vase performance – 4th Round 1982/83

I had a bit deja vu for the final Northern League fixture of the decade i.e. like last Saturday, another journey south of the Tyne with Dekka for a Ryton and Crawcrook Albion away game. Today RACA and us travelled to the former mining town of Easington Colliery in County Durham. The pit here closed in 1993 and the resulting loss of 1,400 jobs had a devastating effect on the area. The football team, known affectionately as The Colliers are still at the heart of the community with a small but loyal support. We did not find their Welfare Park ground straight away, after taking a wrong turn and heading down a dead end street, but we found it second time lucky. Unlike locating the grounds of the top professional clubs, where on a Saturday afternoon you just follow the people wearing the same coloured football tops and you will arrive there, it can sometimes be a bit difficult to find a Northern League ground. There are fewer fans heading to the ground of course and many of these grounds are not very well signposted. Dekka thinks the challenge of travelling to and locating a non-league ground is an enjoyable part of the overall matchday experience. Who am I to argue with this.

Prior to kick off The Colliers were lying 8th in Division 2. RACA were in 3rd place so a close match was anticipated. Dekka and I were both feeling the effects of Christmas excess, him a bit more than me though as he uncharacteristically opted for a pre-match pint of shandy in the clubhouse.

The match kicked off in a strong wind that threatened to spoil it, but it turned out to be a post-Christmas cracker of a contest. RACA had the wind behind them in the first half. They had a couple of early chances, Dan Ord firing over the bar and Dan Blewitt shooting just wide within the first 10 minutes. Easington's first real opportunity came after 20 minutes - Josh Home-Jackson sending his free kick just over the bar. A minute later they had another great chance to take the lead but Jack Brown missed an open goal. It was RACA who finished the half with two more decent chances but Colliers' keeper Alex Lawrence made two good saves to keep it goalless at half time.

RACA made a dream start to the second half when, within the first minute, James Thompson passed to Jack Cooper who fired home his 12th goal of the season. It was then a similar pattern to the first half with end to end stuff. In the first 15 minutes of the second half, the Colliers went close to equalising twice, and both sides had what looked like reasonable claims for penalties turned down (Colliers on 52 minutes and RACA on 58 minutes). On 63 minutes, a well taken goal by RACA's Scott Jasper (also his 12th of the season) gave them a 2-0 lead and with their impressive record of keeping clean sheets in the league this season (9 in 18 matches) it seemed odds on they would see the game out. The Colliers however refused to give up, and 2 minutes later they pulled one back when Kyle Middleton shot through a crowded penalty area and under RACA keeper Josh Graham. In the continuing end to end battle, RACA nearly restored their 2 goal lead, closely followed by the Easington equaliser on 72 minutes – Middleton grabbing his second goal after a scramble in the RACA box. A minute later RACA's Cooper was denied his 13th goal of the season by the post. In the final 15 minutes, both teams had some more chances to win it but it remained level. Dekka and I thought a draw was definitely a fair result, in a non-stop entertaining match and a great advert for non-league football.

Vital Statistics:

Easington Colliery 2 (Middleton 65, 72)
Ryton and Crawcrook Albion 2 (Cooper 46. Jasper 63)

Northern League Division 2

Admission £5

No programmes left when we arrived (due to Easington season ticket holders receiving a free programme and free pint in the clubhouse today to thank them for their support. Nice gesture from the club)

Attendance 105

CESTRIANS BEATEN BY CUMBRIANS IN CLOSE ENCOUNTER
Northern League Ground 35

Saturday 4th January 2020
CHESTER-LE-STREET TOWN
Moor Park, Chester Moor, Chester-le-Street, County Durham

Original club formed in 1920. Played in North Eastern League and Wearside League until they disbanded in 1936.

Current club was established in 1972 as Chester-le-Street Garden Farm. Played in Newcastle City Amateur League and Washington League. Joined the Wearside League in 1977. Dropped Garden Farm from their name in 1978. Promoted to Northern League Division 2 in 1982/83. Won the league in 1983/84 and promoted to Division 1. Relegated back to Division 2 in 1988/89. Have been promoted and relegated 3 times since then - the most recent relegation to Division 2 was 2016/17. Nicknamed The Cestrians.

Northern League Division 2 champions (1983/84, 1997/98)

Best FA Cup performance – 4th Qualifying Round (1986/87)

Best FA Vase performance – 5th Round (1984/85)

For the first Northern League match of the new decade, I made the fairly short trip from Newcastle to watch Chester-le-Street Town. My travelling companion was David Cruise, who was making his second appearance this season (his debut was the 13-0 match at Birtley last October). I met him in Low Fell, Gateshead and after a virtually nearly almost but not quite flawless bus journey (details to remain a secret to spare any embarrassment) we arrived at the ground at 2 pm and had a pre-match pint in the nearby Chester Moor pub. The Cestrians pride themselves on being a family club, and this was certainly borne out by the friendly welcome we received from the volunteers at the gate – although we were both a bit miffed when the young lady taking the admission money asked us if we were concessions. (David is a very young 61 and if she was thinking I am 65 I need to get back into the gym after my Christmas break). Even though it was a very mild afternoon for January, we took the sound advice from the man selling the half-time raffle tickets and sat in the stand with the red plastic seats behind the dugouts (the ground is pretty much open to the elements on the other 3 sides of the pitch).

The visitors today were the Cumbrians of Carlisle City, who were lying 5th in Division 2 before kick-off. Their promotion push had taken a bit of a setback recently (with only 2 points from the last 3 games) so they needed to return to winning ways. Chester-le-Street were in 10th place and at the halfway stage of the season when all teams have played circa 20 matches, they have the distinction of being the only team not to have drawn a match.

The hosts started the brighter and went a goal up after 6 minutes – Owen Henderson shooting low past Carlisle keeper Kyle Townsley. The Cumbrians equalised after 22 minutes, largely against the run of play, when Sam Atkinson found the net after swivelling and shooting from 18 yards out. It was end to end for the remainder of the half and it stayed all square at the interval. The clubhouse was cosy and welcoming for our half-time Bovril.

The Cestrians also started the second half the brighter with a good spell of positive passing play, and on 57 minutes a Michael Hepplewhite goal gave them the lead again. However, a minute later, Jordan Palmer equalised for the Cumbrians straight from the restart. On 72 minutes a Chester-le-Street attack broke down, the ball was cleared upfield and Carlisle's Robert McCartney broke away to shoot past keeper Regan Ward for his 19th goal of the season. The Cestrians fought hard to get back into the game, but the Cumbrians held out to gain a vital win. Ironically, given the Cestrians' lack of draws, we felt a draw would have been the fairest result today in this entertaining close encounter. As we headed back on a bus journey with no hitches, David and I agreed that it had been an enjoyable afternoon at a very friendly club.

Vital Statistics:

Chester-le-Street Town 2 (Henderson 6, Hepplewhite 58)

Carlisle City 3 (Atkinson 22, Palmer 59, McCartney 72)

Northern League Division 2

Admission £5

Programme £1

Attendance 110

WATCHING FOOTBALL AT SOUTH SHIELDS.... EVENTUALLY

Wednesday 8th January 2020
South Shields versus Billingham Town
Mariners Park, Shaftesbury Avenue, South Shields, Tyne and Wear

The coastal town of South Shields lies at the mouth of the River Tyne. I am very familiar with it. Childhood family holidays were spent on the beach there, making the short journey from the family home in Gateshead. It is the finishing point of the Great North Run, the nationally (arguably internationally) renowned half marathon that has been held every September since 1981 (for the record, I have personally ran the 13 miles from Newcastle upon Tyne to South Shields 7 times, gradually taking longer and longer over the years to finish it of course). Last year, the ferry terminal at South Shields marked the completion of the 80 mile Tyne and Wear Heritage Way, that Anita and I had walked in stages. So I know the town pretty well...but until tonight I had never been to a football match there.

There are strong links in football history between South Shields FC and my south side of the Tyne hometown team Gateshead FC. South Shields FC have twice relocated to Gateshead after going bust, in 1930 and 1974. As a teenager, I remember the 1974 occasion well (as recounted in Chapter 3). The current South Shields FC (nicknamed The Mariners) have had remarkable success in the last few years, achieving 3 back to back promotions (Northern League Division 2 champions 2015/16, Northern League Division 1 champions 2016/17 and Northern Premier League Division 1 North champions 2017/18) and winning the FA Vase at Wembley in 2017. Maintaining the Gateshead connection, the current squad includes former Heed players Jon Shaw, Phil Turnbull, Craig Baxter and Josh Gillies (Baxter was playing at right back tonight and Gillies was on the bench but he came on after just 12 minutes following a bad injury to Luke Daly who needed to be stretchered off). The Mariners are currently top of the Northern Premier League Premier Division, a league below Gateshead in National League North, setting up the distinct possibility of them both playing in the same league next season if South Shields win yet another promotion.

The Mariners opponents tonight were Billingham Town (who play 2 levels below in Northern League Division 1) in a Durham Challenge Cup tie (South Shields won this trophy in 2016/17 and were beaten finalists last season – Billingham Town won it in the 2003/04 season). The match was postponed the previous evening due to high winds (on checking Twitter, I found that some fans could not grasp that it is possible for a football match to be called off for this reason) but it was much calmer tonight and I made the fairly last minute spur of the moment decision to drive 11 miles to watch football in South Shields for the first time. The Mariner

Park ground has 2 large covered seated stands (one on either side of the pitch) and covered standing areas behind each goal. It also has a large clubhouse and a separate marquee (I did not go into either of them but they looked impressive). Overall it looks a good set up. I stood on the touchline next to the dugouts, with a good view of the pitch that was well illuminated by the very bright modern floodlights.

South Shields gave some of their youngsters the chance to play alongside some of the regular experienced first team players tonight, and together they made an assured start. After 6 minutes, their striker Lee Mason just failed to get his head to a great cross from Luke Daly but a minute later he opened the scoring with a fine turn and shot from the edge of the box into the bottom corner of the net. Minutes later Daly suffered his unfortunate knee injury as mentioned above. The hosts were in total control in the first half hour and went close twice, before Mason, in space and with time, slotted home his second goal on 34 minutes. Four minutes later Billingham pulled a goal back with a Dan Flounders tap in after a mistake by Mariners' keeper Ross Coombe. Just before half time, Callum Guy restored South Shields' two goal advantage, firing home after a slightly lucky bounce of the ball to him. They started the second half in the same confident manner as the first and continued to press the Billingham goal to kill off the tie. They achieved this on the hour mark when Josh Gillies made it 4-1 when his sublime curling 25 yard shot bulged the net. There was no doubt that the Mariners deserved their lead, with their superior pace and skill throughout the match. However, Billingham never gave up and Luke Hogan scored their second goal on 73 minutes after a well worked move. They went extremely close to scoring a third goal on 83 minutes, when during a goalmouth scramble Mariners' Will Jenkins and Callum Ross both cleared the ball off the goal line. South Shields saw the match out to secure their place in the Quarter Final, that will be another home tie against another Northern League Division 1 team – high flying Stockton Town.

I enjoyed my impromptu trip to this fine ground but weather permitting I will be back trying to complete my Northern League groundhopping Mission within the next few weeks.

Vital Statistics:
South Shields 4 (Mason 7, 34, Guy 46, Gillies 60)
Billingham Town 2 (Flounders 38, Hogan 73)
Durham Challenge Cup 2nd Round
Admission £5
Programme – didn't buy one
Attendance 444

...AND THE LAW WON

Northern League Ground 36

Saturday 18th January 2020
TOW LAW TOWN
Ironworks Road, Tow Law, County Durham

Founded in 1890 and played in the Auckland and District League. Joined the Northern League in 1894 but left again in 1900. After spells in South Durham Alliance, Crook and District League and Auckland and District League again, they re-joined the Northern League in 1920. They have now been in either Division 1 or Division 2 of the Northern League for a century. Nicknamed The Lawyers

Northern League Division 1 champions 1923/24, 1924/25, 1994/95

FA Vase runners up 1997/98

Northern League Cup winners 1973/74

Durham Challenge Cup winners 1895/96

Best FA Cup performance – 2nd Round 1967/68

In 1979, the seminal punk/new wave band The Clash sang 'I Fought The Law (and The Law Won)'. Today saw Brandon United FC fighting The Law (i.e. Tow Law Town FC), and whilst they put up a good fight, The Law certainly won....by 7 goals without reply. Another song by The Clash – 'Complete Control' – would perfectly sum up their performance today.

Learned gentlemen with a much greater knowledge and experience of Northern League football than me (including Kev Larkham and Don at RACA) told me that if I did not visit Tow Law by the end of October I would be lucky to see a match there until March. Given the town's elevated position and the open aspect of The Lawyers' ground, several matches had been postponed during November, December and January due to waterlogged or frozen pitches. In fact, only 2 matches have been completed during this time. The previous Saturday's game against Willington (that I almost went to but am pleased I did not) was abandoned at half time after a farcical first half took place in heavy rain and gale force winds. Today was my lucky day though to tick off The Law – no rain and not very windy (but still extremely cold).

Brandon have had a very tough season so far. Prior to kick off, they were lying rock bottom of Division 2 with only 6 points from 18 games. Ironically, their only league victory this season was over Tow Law back in August. I felt sorry for their few travelling fans (some of whom I stood next to in the second half today) who have been watching some very heavy defeats lately. It did not take The Lawyers long to score the first goal in Brandon's latest heavy defeat, when Jason White escaped his marker in the box and headed home after 9 minutes. He scored his second on 21 minutes, and on 23 minutes a stonewall penalty was converted by Matty Moffat to make it 3-0. Even at this early stage of the match, with the action mainly taking place in their half of the pitch, the visitors must have thought there was no way back. They kept going though and nearly pulled a goal back on the half hour against the run of play, beating the keeper but not the Lawyers' defender who blocked the shot on the goal line. Tow Law remained 3 goals to the good at half time.

Actually physically shivering, I queued during the break at the refreshment window for a Bovril. The man in front of me was disappointed to find out that there were no chips left. When he asked what was available, the man serving replied totally deadpan "burgers…oh and poached salmon in a béarnaise sauce" (one of these turned out to be a lie, I am not saying which one though).

The second half saw Tow Law continue where they left off in the first. White missed an open goal and a chance to compete his hat trick on 50 minutes, and Barrie Smith rattled the bar with a rasping drive after 55 minutes. The inevitable fourth goal arrived on 65 minutes – Jeffrey Smith with a great strike from just outside the penalty area into the bottom left hand corner of the net. On 70 minutes Tow Law were awarded another penalty. I had a very good view of the incident and it was never a penalty ….or as Chris Waddle (who played for Tow Law before his Newcastle, Spurs, England etc career) would say it was never a pelanty. Matty Moffat converted again from the spot. Two minutes later is was 6-0 when Michael Brown scored from the right hand side of the 6 yard box after a good run through the now tiring Brandon defence. In the final minute, Moffat completed his hat trick with a simple tap in, to make it a Magnificent 7 for The Lawyers.

This was the coldest I have felt watching a football match for quite some time, but I thoroughly enjoyed the afternoon at this really good old school type ground.

Vital Statistics:

Tow Law Town 7 (White 9, 21, Moffat 23 pen, 70 pen, 90, Smith 65, Brown 72)
Brandon United 0
Northern League Division 2
Admission £5
Programme – free download
Attendance 40

SYNNERS COULDN'T FIND A WINNER

Northern League Ground 37

Saturday 25th January 2020
BILLINGHAM SYNTHONIA
Norton Sports Complex, Station Road, Norton, Stockton-on-Tees

Established in 1923 as Billingham Synthonia (a contraction of synthetic ammonia that was a product of chemical company ICI who they were affiliated with). Played in South Bank and District League and Teesside League. Joined the Northern League in 1945. Spent majority of seasons since in top flight of Northern League with two relegations from Division 1 to Division 2 (in 1985/86 and 2014/15) followed by quick returns to Division 1. At end of 2017/18 season were relegated to Division 2. Nicknamed The Synners

Northern League Division 1 champions 1956/57, 1988/89, 1989/90, 1995/96

Northern League Division 2 champions 1986/87

Northern League Cup winners 1951/52, 1987/88, 1989/90

Durham Challenge Cup winners 1988/89, 1990/91, 2008/09, 2009/10

North Riding Senior Cup winners 1966/67, 1971/72, 1978/79

Best FA Cup performance – 1st Round 1948/49, 1949/50, 1951/52, 1956/57, 1957/58, 1987/88, 1989/90

Best FA Vase performance – Semi Final 2006/07

Best FA Amateur Cup performance – Quarter Final 1948/49

Best FA Trophy performance – Quarter Final 1993/94

On a mild day for late January, I drove down the A1 to the village of Norton near Stockton on Tees. The Norton Sports Complex is the current temporary home of Billingham Synthonia FC who vacated their Central Avenue stadium in Billingham at the end of the 2016/17 season due to being unable to meet the cost of necessary upgrading work. On arriving at the Complex, it was immediately clear that The Synners are the tenants here. There are signs on the main building stating it is the home of Norton and Stockton Ancients Football Club, Norton Bowling Club, the Billingham Marsh House Harriers, and Hockey Heroes (for the kids). At the entrance gate the only Billingham Synthonia branding in the ground was a sign saying Support The Synners. At most Northern League grounds I have visited over the past 18 months, there has usually been an enticing aroma of sizzling burgers and onions emanating from the clubhouse kitchen or mobile food van. Sad to say this was not the case today though – the fried food smell from the clubhouse was not very tempting so I stayed outside.

Today's opponents were West Allotment Celtic who like me travelled due south from the Newcastle upon Tyne area. Unlike me, some of their players were travelling via the A19 where planned major roadworks were causing traffic delays, making them late for the kick off. It was agreed to wait for them to arrive and the match eventually got underway at 3.17 pm. How different from Premier League football. Allotment were flying high at the top of Division 2 before today's proceedings, 8 points ahead of 2nd placed Redcar Athletic with 2 games in hand. Synners were lying 7th, had been on decent form recently, and were only 3 points away from the 4th place promotion spot. I was anticipating a good contest and it did not disappoint.

Both teams started brightly (straight out of the blocks, really going for it – to use football TV commentator-speak) and had early chances to open the scoring. It was non-stop action with good attacking and defending from both. The first half looked like ending goalless until there was a goal fest in the last 7 minutes of it. Shane Jones opened the scoring for the visitors on 38 minutes – bending the ball from the edge of the box into the top corner of the goal. Two minutes later Chris Dickinson coolly despatched a penalty to bring Synners level. Just before the break, Matthew Wilson gave Synners a 2-1 lead with a neat lob over Allotment keeper Finlay Hodgson.

The Allotment half time team talk had an immediate desired effect when Jones grabbed his second goal on 47 minutes. However Synners then took control of this enthralling contest for the next half hour. They had the greater share of possession and went close to taking the lead again a few times, but they just could not find the winner against Allotment's resolute defence. I must admit I got a bit caught up in the euphoria of their numerous attacks, running to retrieve the ball 3 times when it landed near to me and quickly kicking/throwing it back to a Synner. In the last 10 minutes both teams were starting to tire a bit. It looked like ending in 'a Desmond' when with 2 minutes left Jones squared the ball in the penalty box to Shane Donaghey who slotted it home to give Allotment a 3-2 victory. It was a bit tough on The Synners who I felt deserved a point at the very least for their efforts today. Allotment did not have it easy but they proved they can grind out a win (similar to runaway Premier League leaders Liverpool who have managed to win games this season when they haven't been at their best). I fully expect to see West Allotment Celtic and Liverpool still at the top of their respective leagues at the end of the season.

This was an absolutely cracking match and a great advert for Northern League football.

Vital Statistics:

Billingham Synthonia 2 (Dickinson 40 pen, Wilson 43)
West Allotment Celtic 3 (Jones 38, 47, Donaghey 88)

Northern League Division 2

Admission £6

Programme £1

Attendance 86

..........SECOND MISSION......COMPLETION IN SIGHT.......

TERRIERS FIND THEIR BARK AND BITE

Northern League Ground 38

Saturday 1st February 2020
BEDLINGTON TERRIERS
Dr. Pit Welfare Park, Park Road, Bedlington, Northumberland

Founded in 1949 as Bedlington Mechanics. Played in Northumberland Miners Welfare League, Northern Combination and Northern Alliance. Disbanded in 1963 but reformed in 1965 as Bedlington Colliery Welfare and played in Northern Alliance. In 1979 joined the Tyneside Amateur League as Bedlington United, then re-joined Northern Alliance as Bedlington Terriers in 1980. One of the founder members of Northern League Division 2 in 1982, promoted to Division 1 (1984/85), relegated back to Division 2 (1986/87), then promoted to Division 1 again (1993/94). The most successful spell in their history followed (see honours below). At end of 2015/16 season they were relegated to Division 2. Nicknamed The Terriers

Northern League Division 1 champions - 1997/98, 1998/99, 1999/2000, 2000/01, 2001/02

Northern League Division 2 champions – 1993/94

Northern League Cup winners – 1996/97, 2000/01

Northumberland Senior Cup winners – 1996/97, 1997/98, 2001/02, 2003/04

Best FA Cup performance – 2nd Round 1998/99

Best FA Vase performance – Runners up 1998/99

On this bright but windy Saturday, Robbo and I headed into Northumberland to watch Bedlington Terriers FC. Life had not been too good for the Terriers lately, both on and off the field. On it they had lost their last 5 games, and off it their floodlights were out of order meaning the kick off today was moved forward an hour to 2 pm. In 2010 the Terriers received sponsorship from Robert E Rich Jr. (the American billionaire owner of Rich Products Corporation – a frozen food manufacturer) after his wife discovered ancestral links to the town of Bedlington. His investment in the club included the purchase of a very impressive £30,000 electronic scoreboard that, unlike the floodlights, was still in perfect working order today. It seemed a bit flamboyant for the Northern League but the rest of the ground was in the same vein of what I have generally witnessed in the last 18 months of groundhopping around this league. There is a large stand with flip seats and standing areas, a decent clubhouse and food hut, and a sign above the entrance to the changing rooms saying 'Woof Woof Terriers, Who Let The Dogs Out'.

The visitors today were Easington Colliery FC so it was Terriers versus Colliers. It was also both teams versus a strong wind. Easington had the wind behind them in the first half but Bedlington defended resolutely and restricted The Colliers to a few half chances that they could not convert. The Terriers looked happy to go into the break level but I still expected The Colliers to find the net in the second half and condemn The Terriers to a 6th straight defeat. I was to be proved spectacularly wrong.

Bedlington, with the wind now behind them, had a second half game plan of hoofing the ball over the Easington defence to their 2 strikers and it worked like a dream. They opened the scoring on 54 minutes with their first shot of the match (scorer Malik Kalimba). Five minutes later, another long ball over the defence found David Allason and he slotted it past Colliers' keeper Chris Rookes. Terriers' third goal saw the long ball played from Allason to Kalimba, who beat Rookes in a one on one. Kalimba completed his hat trick on 80 minutes after a defensive error. Even the Bedlington fans and officials near to us could hardly believe their team's second half performance as they celebrated a win for the first time since mid-December. Football really is a funny old game.

Vital Statistics:

Bedlington Terriers 4 (Kalimba 54, 70, 80, Allason 59) Easington Colliery 0
Northern League Division 2
Admission £5
Programme - none
Attendance 50

Wednesday 4th March 2020
Heaton Stannington v West Allotment Celtic
Grounsell Park, Newton Road, High Heaton, Newcastle upon Tyne, NE7 7HP

I had hoped to tick off Jarrow FC tonight to complete The Second Mission. Unfortunately, their ground failed a lunchtime pitch inspection and their match against Bedlington Terriers was called off. I had 3 of their home games in mind during February but all were called off due to a waterlogged pitch. Frustrating for sure, but with 10 home games still to play by the end of April, there would be more than enough matches to choose from to pay them a visit.

Robbo and I went to Grounsell Park instead for Heaton Stannington's match against local rivals West Allotment Celtic. It was a clash of 2 teams vying for promotion to Division 1. The Stan were 7th prior to kick-off but only 2 points away from a promotion place. Allotment were sitting 4 points clear at top of the table with 2 games in hand over their closest challengers.

A fiery close encounter was anticipated and it proved to be a tight and goalless first half. Both sides had a few chances to break the deadlock but the defences held sway. In the 20 to 30 minute period there were some poor tackles going in from Allotment, leading to yellow cards for Abu Salim and Jacob Forster. This is the third time I have watched Allotment this season and, whilst there is no doubt that they are one of the top teams in this league, they have been very physical and prone to niggly fouls in all 3 matches.

In the second half, The Stan took an early lead with a goal that striker Lee Middleton wanted to claim (naturally) but was officially chalked up as an own goal by Allotment skipper Jack Errington. The goal seemed to spark the visitors to forget the rough stuff and start to play some football. On 53 minutes their prolific striker Matthew Hayton beat two Stan defenders and slid the ball home. Both sides were not settling for the draw and looking to find the winner. Stan thought they had found it on 78 minutes when an amazing strike from just outside the penalty area by Regan Paterson took everyone in the ground, including Allotment keeper Finlay Hodgson, by surprise and made it 2-1. It was a fantastic goal that really deserved to win any match.... but sadly for The Stan not this one. Allotment equalised for the second time on 82 minutes via a great finish from Hayton. It finished 2-2 and I suppose both sides will be happy not to have lost, to keep their promotion hopes alive in what looks to be an exciting battle among up to 8 teams in the run in.

Vital Statistics:

Heaton Stannington 2 (Errington og 47, Paterson 78)
West Allotment Celtic 2 (Hayton 53, 82)
Northern League Division 2
Admission £5
No programmes left when we arrived just before kick-off
Attendance 241

RAM RAID AT MARINE

Saturday 14th March 2020
Marine v Ramsbottom United
Marine Travel Arena, Rossett Park, College Road, Crosby, Merseyside

My original plan for this weekend was to go to watch my hometown team Gateshead FC for the first time this season with my brother Kev, who as previously mentioned lives in Liverpool. I took the train from Newcastle to Liverpool on Friday afternoon as confirmation was coming through that all Premier League and EFL matches were being cancelled for at least 3 weeks due to the escalating coronavirus situation. The National League held a long meeting that afternoon which resulted in the decision to go ahead with matches in its 3 Divisions this weekend – including therefore Gateshead's away game at Southport in the National League North. That evening though this match was postponed due to the Gateshead players having to self-isolate.

A couple of years ago I would probably have just shrugged my shoulders and did something non-football related with Kev in Liverpool instead – anything from visiting a museum (highbrow) to a pub crawl (low brow). However, I have now become much more groundhopper-ish and the golden rule for any good hardy groundhopper would be to try to find another suitable match to attend. The Northern Premier League Division 1 North West (Level 8) games were allowed to go ahead and we decided to make the short 20 minute train journey from Liverpool to Crosby to watch Marine FC versus Ramsbottom United. They were 3rd and 2nd respectively in the table before kick off (both on 58 points, Ramsbottom had a +1 better goal difference) and both were realistically trying to secure a promotion playoff place (given that league leaders Workington were 10 points clear of them in the one automatic promotion place).

The club volunteers who greeted us at the gate were typical friendly scousers who were very appreciative that we had decided to visit the club today. We had a pre-match pint in the excellent clubhouse that was located behind one of the goals at the turnstile end. The only seated area in the ground was also located behind this goal – a good sized stand with black and white seats (the white seats spelling out MAFC).

There was uncovered terracing behind the other goal. On the side of the pitch where the dugouts were, there was no spectator access at all. There were very tall nets on this side to stop loose balls ending up in the back gardens of the houses behind. They were partially successful today (we counted at least 3 times when balls cleared the nets). There was a cowshed type covered standing area along the whole length of the touchline opposite the dugouts and we stood here with a mix of Marine and Ramsbottom (aka Rammy) supporters.

The match was as close as the league positions suggested it would be. Tight marking and good defending were the main features of a goalless first half. It could have been a different story if a poor foul after 10 minutes by Marine's James Devine near to the touchline right next to where we were standing received a red card rather than the yellow one it was given (we had a great view and reckon it was borderline).

The match opened up a bit in the second half. Both teams had chances to break the deadlock. Marine in particular were guilty of some woeful finishing in and around the six yard box on 3 occasions. In the last 2 seasons, I had been to 52 matches (43 new grounds) and had never witnessed a 0-0. It was beginning to look like that proud record was in jeopardy today. When Jamie Rother came on as sub for Rammy on 84 minutes I said to Kev that he was my last hope – a striker with a fresh pair of legs. On 88 minutes he duly obliged, sending a great volley into the net from Eddie Cooper's cross. The Rammy players forgot the current social distancing non-contact recommendations and piled on each other near the corner flag. Rammy fans celebrated beating their promotion rivals at the death more in line with Government guidelines but celebrate they certainly did.

We thoroughly enjoyed this visit to a well-run friendly non-league club, but as we headed back to Liverpool, we wondered whether there would be any more football taking place this season after this weekend's matches.

Vital Statistics:

Marine 0 Ramsbottom United 1 (Rother 88)
Northern Premier League Division 1 North West
Admission £10
Attendance 677

STOPPAGE TIME
Lockdown 2020

The Marine versus Ramsbottom United match did turn out to be the last one I attended in the 2019/20 season. With the finish line in sight to complete The Second Mission and therefore The Overall Mission for Northern League Divisions 1 and 2, I was suddenly stopped in my tracks. Due to the increasing spread of coronavirus, it was initially decided on 13th March that all Northern League fixtures were suspended until at least 3rd April. This proved to be optimistic, and when the UK entered lockdown on 23rd March it was decided to end the current Northern League season with all results expunged and no promotion or relegation. The Northern League was not unique of course - all football in the UK was halted. The main debate from groundhoppers on social media was whether matches attended during the season in leagues where results had been expunged could still be counted as valid ground ticks. My view and the general consensus was that they could.

Northern League Ground 39
WASHINGTON
New Ferens Park , Belmont, Durham

Original club was formed in early 20th Century by miners from the Washington F-Pit Colliery and known as Washington Colliery. Played in the North Eastern League. Present incarnation of the club was established after the World War II in 1947 as Washington Colliery Mechanics. Played in Washington and District League and Northern Alliance. In 1965 changed name to Washington FC, joined the Wearside League and then the Northern League. Runners up in Northern League Division 2 at end of 2014/15 season and promoted to Division 1. Financial difficulties and relegation back to Division 2 followed. Club had to vacate their Albany Park home ground in 2010/11 and play at Nissan Sports Ground. At start of 2019/20 season they moved to new temporary home - New Ferens Park ground in Durham. Nickname The Mechanics

As detailed in Chapter 8, I went to a Durham Ladies match in 2019 at New Ferens Park that is the current temporary home of Washington FC – perennial nomads since 2011. I perfectly reasonably counted this as a ground ticked off with no need to re-visit it. This meant that with only Jarrow FC left to visit The Overall Mission was confirmed as 97.5% complete (39 ground ticks out of 40). But for the time being, it was stoppage time. Not merely the few minutes stoppage time that frequently occurs when players are injured or substitutions are made of course – or less frequently when there is a streaker on the pitch or (generally in non-league football) when the floodlights fail. This extended football hiatus meant that The Overall Mission could not be completed until the 2020/21 season.

The late Bill Shankly, who managed Liverpool FC from 1959 to 1974, famously once said 'Some people think football is a matter of life and death. I don't like that attitude. I can assure them it is much more serious than that'. This was typical Shankly wit and, of course, it was tongue in cheek. The coronavirus pandemic was an unprecedented situation; the furthest away from normal life that the UK had been since the Second World War. No reasonable person would suggest that football is more important than life and death. Football is important to millions of fans in the UK though. To have the normality of being able to attend a football match suddenly taken away was a very strange feeling for me and I am sure for millions of others. I fully appreciate that there were more serious consequences of lockdown than not being able to watch football. Thousands of people in the UK tragically lost their lives to coronavirus. Everyone felt the economic and social consequences of it in some way. Elderly more vulnerable people were not able to leave their homes at all for 3 months, and children were denied their regular school attendance routines. But, like many other football fans I know, I was missing it and I vowed to appreciate the simple pleasure of going to the match even more when it returned.

A GAME OF NO CROWDS

During April the only football you could watch was on TV – and that was merely re-runs of recent and not so recent matches – classics from previous World Cups, Euros, Play-off Finals etc. It was enjoyable watching some great old matches of course but it was no substitute for watching a live football match. I was starting to hanker for standing on a windswept terrace on a cold winter's night in some Godforsaken part of County Durham!

On 16th May, the Bundesliga in Germany resumed in strict safety conditions, behind closed doors with no spectators. In the same way, the English Premier League restarted on 17th June, followed by the English Championship and FA Cup matches. The UEFA Champions League and Europa League competitions were competed in August – still behind closed doors. The resumption of non-league behind closed doors football started in July. Gateshead (my south side of the Tyne) qualified for the National League North Play Offs following a Points Per Game calculation. On Sunday 19th July they beat Brackley Town on penalties in the Quarter Final, but sadly lost 5-3 to Boston United in a cracking Semi Final match on Saturday 25th July to remain in the second top tier of non-league football for the 2020/21 season. Anita and I watched these Two Games of No Crowds at home via a subscription channel on our laptop.

The restart saw Newcastle United (my north side of the Tyne) pull away from the Premier League relegation zone. They finished 13th when the season eventually ended on Sunday 26th July. Off the field there had been serious talk during the lockdown of Mike Ashley selling the club to a Saudi Arabian consortium, but on Thursday 30th July it was announced that the proposed purchase had fallen through so the Ashley regime continues at St James' Park.

EXTRA TIME

On Wednesday 19th August, it was announced that clubs in the lower levels of the English Football Pyramid, including the two Divisions of the Northern League, could allow spectators back in to watch matches, subject to complying with set coronavirus safety instructions. The maximum number of fans at Northern League games was to be 300. Of course, many clubs, particularly in Division 2, can only dream of having crowds anywhere near that figure.

On Wednesday 2nd September, 172 days since the last football match I attended at Marine FC, Robbo and I went to Grounsell Park for Heaton Stannington's Extra Preliminary Qualifying Round FA Cup tie against West Auckland Town. The attendance was 261 (a great turnout on a particularly rainy evening), and on the whole social distancing was observed. The Stan's Road to Wembley Glory started at 7.30 pm and finished just short of two hours later when a 95th minute goal by West Auckland's Adam Mitchell gave them a 3-2 win in a pulsating cup tie. There's always next season Stan!

It felt great to be watching football again and I could at last continue The Overall Mission. My Game of Two Halves was about to enter a short period of extra time.

ENDGAME

Northern League Ground 40

Saturday 12th September 2020
JARROW
Perth Green, Jarrow, Tyne and Wear

Original club formed in 1894 and played in Northern Alliance. Disbanded at end of 1901/02 season. Reformed and re-joined Northern Alliance in 1903. In 1910/11 joined North Eastern League as Jarrow Croft. In 1918 renamed Palmers Jarrow. Changed name to Jarrow FC in 1920. In 1945 re-joined Northern Alliance. In 1949 dropped down to Northern Combination and then disbanded again. Current club was formed in 1980 and played in Wearside League. Champions in 2016/17 and promoted to Northern League Division 2

The Second Mission and therefore The Overall Mission, that I had expected to complete around 6 months earlier during the 2019/20 season, was at last completed on the second weekend of the new 2020/21 season on Saturday 12th September 2020.

With face mask on and observing social distancing, I made the short Metro journey to Jarrow for their game against Durham City. At the turnstile, the current new normal way of entering a non-league football ground was in full operation. After leaving my personal details for the track and trace system and using the hand sanitiser, I was cleared to enter. Despite the tremendous efforts of the officials, players and volunteers at the clubs, the coronavirus was still having an impact on some Northern League fixtures. On the opening day of the season last Saturday (5th September) and during midweek, 8 matches had been postponed due to players testing positive for the virus. It is of course impossible for the part-time playing squads of Northern League clubs to be kept in bio secure bubbles like the Premier League squads are, so it seems highly likely that games being called off for this reason will be ongoing throughout the season. I sense it could be a tough road ahead.

Jarrow had added Lee Kerr to their squad last season. A vastly experienced midfielder at Northern League level, he has 3 FA Vase winners' medals from his time at Whitley Bay, and he has been a steadying influence on Jarrow's young players. In the close season Durham City made the surprising appointment of former Celtic player Didier Agathe as manager, and they have brought in many new players including some from overseas. After two games played so far this season, both teams were looking for their first win today.

My companion at this final Northern League ground tick was Robbo, who I met inside the ground. It was a lovely day to watch football – calm and mild – and the pitch was in early season perfect condition (I was finding it hard to believe that this was the same playing surface that had been constantly waterlogged during February pre-lockdown preventing me from completing The Mission then). The pre-match entertainment was provided by a border collie being allowed onto the pitch to chase the warming up players and round up footballs instead of sheep.

The game was an entertaining affair, with both teams trying to play good attacking football throughout. Jarrow scored first after 15 minutes when a rasping penalty kick from Liam McBryde that hit the bar, was followed up and tucked away by Adam Lennox. Durham equalised on the half hour when a great through ball from D'Andre Wainwright was neatly fired into the net by Abdul Wahab. Jarrow took the lead again just before half time – Lennox scoring his second. After the interval, the home side were in the ascendency looking for the killer third goal. They were denied by some good but sometimes last-ditch desperate defending, and in particular by some fine saves from Durham keeper Quinaceo Hunt. On 73 minutes, Durham went down to 10 men when Maurice Kone received a straight red card card for a last man professional foul. It felt like it was game over for Durham then, and the Jarrow victory was sealed on 83 minutes when Adam Lennox completed his hat trick (by this point in the match we were having some craic with Adam's dad Kev, who was standing near to us giving his son some words of encouragement from pitch side). Durham's new look team certainly have some skill in their ranks but they have not quite gelled together yet. Their first win will not be too far away though.

Vital Statistics:

Jarrow 3 (Lennox 15, 42, 83) Durham City 1 (Wahab 29)

Northern League Division 2

Admission £5

Programme £1

Attendance 129

……SECOND MISSION…….ACCOMPLISHED…….

......AND THE OVERALL MISSION.....ACCOMPLISHED.....

The final whistle was blown on my Northern League groundhopping journey. It had started in August 2018 at Sunderland RCA, and via Shildon, Dunston UTS, Newcastle Benfield, West Auckland Town, Ryhope Colliery Welfare, Whickham, North Shields, Ashington, Seaham Red Star, Consett, Guisborough Town, Bishop Auckland, Newton Aycliffe, Ryton and Crawcrook Albion, Heaton Stannington, Whitley Bay, Hebburn Town, Penrith, West Allotment Celtic, Stockton Town, Durham City, Willington, Newcastle University, Billingham Town, Northallerton Town, Crook Town, Redcar Athletic, Brandon United, Birtley Town, Esh Winning, Carlisle City, Thornaby, Sunderland West End, Easington Colliery, Chester-le-Street Town, Tow Law Town, Billingham Synthonia, Bedlington Terriers and Washington, it had finished 2 years later at Jarrow.

I had travelled circa 2,100 miles door to door to complete The Mission. Altogether I had been to 44 matches where at least one team playing was from the Northern League, with 180 total goals scored (4.09 per game) and I had not witnessed a goalless draw. I felt like having an open-topped bus celebration but settled for opening a bottle of pretend champagne (i.e. prosecco) with Anita that evening instead.

As any groundhopper worth their salt will tell you, it is an ongoing pursuit. I am now an enthusiastic 'hopper and have plans to visit many more grounds particularly in Northern England and Scotland (and beyond once it becomes a bit easier to travel abroad again after the coronavirus pandemic hopefully comes completely to an end). I will write about these next adventures in my blog;

The Casual Bystander - https://wordpress.com/home/stout-hearted.blog

and who knows these match reports may form the basis of a follow up book to *My Game of Two Halves*. Maybe I could call it *The Third Half*? Mathematicians would of course argue that you can only have two halves not three, but it would again be a book about football not maths!

POST-MATCH
Many thanks!

Whether it is the pundits on TV and radio or the punters in the pub, when three short blasts of the referee's whistle signals the game is over, it is time for the post-match analysis to begin. I hope, dear reader, that when you conduct your own post-match analysis of *My Game of Two Halves* that you have enjoyed it (or at least some of it) and have found some empathy with my reminiscences of watching football over the years. I thank you for reading it.

I would like to sincerely thank Celtic supporting Vince Ryan (a friend for over 25 years) for his great work on the design, layout and formatting prior to publishing the book that you now have in your hands or on your electronic reading device.

Like the Time Lord Doctor Who had his Sarah Jane, Romana, Rose Tyler etc. I have enjoyed the company of numerous travelling companions on the groundhopping journeys in The Second Half – my lovely wife Anita, the 2 Kevs (my brother and Mr. Larkham), Ken Richardson, Mark, David 'Robbo' Robinson, Derek 'Dekka' Muse, David Cruise, Vince and Caroline Ryan, Alan, and Tenerife Dave. My grateful thanks to these hardy souls for sharing the experience enthusiastically, and I hope that they will take any comments made about them in the good-natured way that I intended them to be.

To help the flow of the narrative in The First Half of the book, I have tended to refer to fellow Newcastle and Gateshead fans I have attended games with generically as friends, rather than state their full names. This also applies to friends from Scotland. I am no less grateful for the part they have played in this football love match.